Occupy the Economy

"Capitalism has hit the fan and now, thanks to the decisions by and for the 1 percent, we're now mired in the Second Great Depression. In this accessible and engaging set of interviews, Richard Wolff explains the tremendous damage inflicted upon the 99 percent in trying to fix the mounting problems by attempting to reform capitalism and how the movement to occupy the economy can move us in a healthier, more democratic direction—beyond capitalism."
—David F. Ruccio, Professor of Economics, University of Notre Dame

"Richard Wolff lays out a compelling framework for further anti-corporate organizing that focuses on the root of the problem: capitalism and its never-ending assault on the 99%. Occupiers (past, present, and future) now have an intellectual guide to a different kind of economy—one that's equitable, sustainable and, let's hope, politically achievable, sooner rather than later. Wolff's deep but conversational synthesis of recent practice and older theory couldn't be more timely, persuasive, and readable." —Steve Early, labor activist, journalist, and author of *The Civil Wars in U.S. Labor*

Occupy the Economy
CHALLENGING CAPITALISM

Richard Wolff
Interviews with David Barsamian

Open Media Series
City Lights Books

The Open Media Series is edited by Greg Ruggiero and archived by
the Tamiment Library, New York University.

eISBN 978-0-87286-568-6 (ebook)

Library of Congress Cataloging-in-Publication Data

Wolff, Richard.
 Occupy the economy : challenging capitalism / by Richard Wolff ; interviews
with David Barsamian.
     p. cm. — (Open media series)
 ISBN 978-0-87286-567-9 (paper)
1. United States—Economic conditions—2009- 2. United States—
Economic policy—2009- 3. Capitalism—United States. 4. Income
distribution—United States. 5. Occupy movement. I. Barsamian, David. II.
Title.

 HC106.84.W65 2012
 339.20973—dc23

                              2012006793

City Lights Books are published at the City Lights Bookstore,
261 Columbus Avenue, San Francisco, CA 94133.
www.citylights.com

Contents

Introduction

For the last half-century, capitalism has been a taboo subject in the United States. Among politicians, journalists, and academics—and in public conversation generally—the word has been avoided or else exclusively praised in over-the-top prose. Professional economists have used words like "perfect competition" and "optimal allocation of resources" and "efficiency" to teach their students and assure one another how absolutely wonderful capitalism was for everyone. Politicians repeated, robot-style, that the "U.S. is the greatest country in the world" and that "capitalism is the greatest economic system in the world." Those few who have dared to raise questions or criticisms about capitalism have been either ignored or told to go live in North Korea, China or Cuba as if that were the only alternative to pro-capitalism cheerleading.

Americans have criticized and debated their educational, medical, welfare, transportation, mass media, political, and many other institutions and systems. They have questioned and at least partly transformed such traditional institutions as racism, sexism, the heterosexual family and the state. They have even sometimes challenged this or that aspect of the economy such as prices, Federal Reserve actions, and so on, but almost never the particular economic system.

Questioning and criticizing capitalism have been taboo, treated by federal authorities, immigration officials, police and most of the public alike as akin to treason. Fear-driven silence has substituted for the necessary, healthy criticism without which all institutions, systems, and traditions harden into dogmas, deteriorate into social rigidities, or worse. Protected from criticism and debate, capitalism in the United States could and has indulged all its darker impulses and tendencies. No public exposure, criticism and movement for change could arise or stand in its way as the system and its effects became ever more unequal, unjust, inefficient and oppressive. Long before the Occupy movement arose to reveal and oppose what U.S. capitalism had become, that capitalism had divided the 1 percent from the 99 percent.

The importance of the Occupy movement was and is positioning its challenge to capitalism front and center among its concerns and passions. No oppositional mass movement of the last fifty years—one drawing broadly inclusive participation—has been similarly daring in going beyond single-issue focus to make economic injustice for the 99 percent *and* the ruling economic system central, defining issues. Despite the power of pro-capitalism ideology, Occupy has been able to contest it in amazingly profound ways in an amazingly short time and for an amazing number of Americans.

Of course Occupy is a first step. Nothing of comparably broad scope and with such transformative social objectives has ever moved forward in a straight line. It's rather two steps forward, one step backward. However a major barrier has been broken, a major line crossed, and a new stage of U.S. politics has begun. The issue of our economic system and whether it is adequate to our needs as a people has now been returned to the center of national discussion, criticism, and debate.

The political, mass media, and academic establishments react predictably. They can not acknowledge the historic significance of what Occupy says and does; that would require admitting the need to debate precisely those issues they had effectively banned from acceptable public discourse. So the politicians repress. New York's Mayor Bloomberg claimed that he forcibly removed Occupy from Zuccotti Park for reasons of cleanliness. Bloomberg, it should be remembered, has presided for many years over one of the filthiest subway systems in the industrial world, one of the dirtiest public garbage systems, and a snow removal system that inspires only our leading comics. The mass media did their usual bit: ignoring Occupy as long as possible, massively misreporting when Occupy was hot news, largely cheering or glossing the removal of Occupy encampments, and then resuming the basic practice of ignoring the ongoing developments of Occupy and related events and activities.

The academic economics profession ought to have been most intimately involved in analyzing and debating a broken capitalist system whose deep crisis had confounded all its confident expectations. It has done nothing of the sort. Instead it proceeds as if—and indeed mostly still insists that nothing has happened to disturb its fifty-year celebration of capitalism's efficiency and growth. A few professors of economics (e.g., Paul Krugman) and business (e.g., Nouriel Roubini) have commented on the absurdity of that insistence. But most of them could get no further than to recycle Keynes' 1930s critiques of a depressed capitalism and his recommendations for deficit spending and monetary stimuli by the government. And, of course, the few right-wing economists who have taken the crisis seriously, utilized it to push yet again for less government economic intervention as the panacea.

Questioning the system and debating basic system change has remained—for government, mainstream media and most professors—something beyond the pale. They see no need to end their 50-year repression or marginalization of such questions and debates. For them, the basic organizations of production and distribution of commodities, like the property and power structures that sustain them, do not deserve criticism. Yet the pressure and mass constituency for a real challenge to that repression had been building across the crisis and emerged with public power in the Occupy movement in late 2011.

The interviews gathered in this book further contest that repression and further develop that challenge. As a broad array of questions are raised and discussed, one theme becomes ever clearer. The failure of government regulation, the growing inequalities of income and wealth, the roll-back on New Deal reforms, the parallel impositions of mass austerity programs by European and U.S. governments: these and many more aspects of the crisis that hit in 2007 are shown to result from how the capitalist system works and not only from this or that particular historical event or economic actor.

Across the pages that follow, what emerges is the central importance of how capitalism very particularly organizes production: masses of working people generate corporate profits that others take and use. Tiny boards of directors, selected by and responsible to tiny groups of major shareholders, gather and control corporate profits, thereby shaping and dominating society. That tiny minority (boards and major shareholders) of those associated with and dependent upon corporations make all the basic decisions—how, what, and where to produce and what to do with the profits. The vast majority of workers within and residents surrounding those capitalist corporations must live with the results of corporate decisions. Yet they are systematically excluded from participating in making those decisions. Nothing more glaringly contradicts democracy than how capitalism organizes the corporate enterprises where working people produce the goods and services without which modern life *for everyone* would be impossible.

On the one hand, criticism and debate around the adequacy of capitalism in relation to real alternatives have been repressed in the United States and beyond. On the other hand, the evidence this book considers shows that we need that criticism and debate now more than ever. The interviews therefore do not shy away from posing the logical and reasonable questions flowing from the topics covered: Does capitalism serve the interests of most people? Can we do better than capitalism?

Nor do the interviews hesitate to suggest some logical answers to questions such as: It is possible to democratize the economy? And is it possible to advance society beyond capitalism?

Key steps in building a social movement in that direction are the psychological as well as ideological breakthroughs to activism being achieved by the Occupy movement. A next step entails working through the ideas, concepts, principles, and values needed to empower, mobilize, grow, and unify the emerging activist generation. This book seeks to contribute to that next step.

Preoccupations

Santa Fe, New Mexico, September 12, 2011

You write that "we had a remarkable 150 years during which workers enjoyed a steadily rising standard of living." When and why did that stop?

The remarkable thing about U.S. history that distinguishes it in many ways from almost every other experiment in capitalist systems is that every decade from 1820 to 1970 the real wage kept rising. Real wage simply means the money you get, adjusted for the prices you have to pay. There's probably no other capitalism that delivered to its working class that kind of remarkable 150-year history that produced this sense that every generation will live better than the one before.

Before I answer your question about why it stopped, just consider for a moment the trauma that it must represent to a population of Americans that have become used to the idea that we live in a charmed land that delivers a wonderful, rising standard of well-being for American working people. For many it represents the end of a world, the end of a set of expectations, the end of a notion of a good future that will come as the reward for hard work. And the trauma is all the worse when there's no honest discussion of it and no easy way to connect with others who are having a similar experience.

Why has it happened? As all major phenomena in human history, it has many reasons, many causes. But I'm going to select four of them that I think were key. The first two have to do with the offering of jobs. That is, in our system new jobs depend on the decisions of private employers as to whether or not it is profitable to hire people. In the 1970s American employers did two things that made them need and want fewer employees.

The first one was a technological breakthrough called the computer, which made it possible for employers to reduce the number of people hired because the computers could now do much more. The simplest example is to remember that once upon a time supermarkets needed an army of workers to keep track of how many much cereal, soup, paper cups and so on were leaving the shelves. With a computer, as we all now know, you have a scanner at the checkout counter, and nobody needs to keep track of it. There's one person sitting at a computer somewhere in the middle of nowhere who can tell you exactly how many new boxes have to be ordered, in which supermarket, in what town, because it's all done automatically and you don't need an army of inventory replacers.

The second thing that happened in the 1970s was the

recognition and the decision of U.S. employers that the national wage level, which had been rising for all these years, was much higher than in other countries, and it would be more profitable to move production to those parts of the world. Between the computer replacing people and the jobs being internationally outsourced, the demand for labor in the U.S. shrank.

At the same time, two other phenomena also contributed. The first was the U.S. women's movement to join the work force. Starting in the 1970s, millions of American housewives decided to add the role of paid worker. At the same time, we had the latest influx of people from Latin America arriving in search of a job and a better life. So a reduction in the demand for jobs by employers and an increase in the number of people looking for work—women and immigrants—occurred at the same time in the 1970s. For the first time in U.S. history there was no labor shortage. We had a system that was successful as a form capitalism. Employers were making money, wanted to grow their businesses and were hiring. But there was always a shortage and that opened the door for immigrants.

In the 1970s, U.S. capitalists discovered that it was no longer necessary to raise wages: they had less need for workers and more people looking for jobs. And every capitalist in the U.S. realized what many had learned at M.B.A. school could be put into effect, namely, the great lesson that if you don't have to raise the wages of your workers, don't do it. You make more money. That's what U.S. employers have been doing for more than 30 years now.

According to the Bureau of Labor Statistics in Washington, which keeps these records, the average wage earned by an American worker in 2011 is about what it was in 1978. We've had thirty-plus years in which the real wage, on average, hasn't improved in the United States. That is a sea change in our history. Meanwhile the last thirty years also saw rising worker productivity; workers were producing ever more for their employers to sell while their employers gave them no more for their work.

Something also is going on parallel to wages flattening out. I believe American workers work more hours than any other work force in the world. Is that right?

That's right. According to the OECD, an important data-gathering service for industrialized countries, Americans do more hours of paid labor per year than any other working class in any advanced industrial country. To keep alive the American dream and the hope of delivering a better life to their families and children, American workers have been working more. Men started taking second jobs. The women, I've already mentioned, left the home and entered the work force. Retired people have come out of retirement to help the family, and teenagers began working on weekends. At the same time, people are being constantly bombarded by advertising that define success in America as having a better house, a better car, a better vacation and a better college education for their children. To keep up with the pressure, people began working more and more.

And, of course, the other new thing the U.S. working class began to do was take on debt. One way to keep your consumption and standard of living rising when your wages are not is to borrow. Starting in the 1970s, working people in the U.S. borrowed money on a scale that has never been seen before in any country. Capitalists began devising new mechanisms for providing credit to the mass of people. Prior to that time, the only people who carried a plastic credit card in their wallets were businessmen working off an expense account. But in the 1970s all that changed. Banks began pumping credit cards into everybody's hands as fast as they could. New business formed—MasterCard, Visa and all the rest—to make mass credit available to people.

So at this time you have wages flattening out, hours and productivity soaring, and huge individual debt accumulating, as if the banks are saying, "No problem, we'll lend to you, easy credit," and then they charge usurious rates.

The amazing thing about the last thirty years is the degree to which there was a kind of collective self-delusion in the United States around the issue of borrowing. It's not rocket science to know that if your wages aren't going up and you keep borrowing to consume, you will soon reach a point where you cannot cover the interest and repayment costs of your debt.

By 2007 the American working class had accumulated a level of debt that was no longer sustainable. People just couldn't make the payments anymore. The bubble began to burst. It's a crisis that really began in the 1970s, when the wages stopped going up, a crisis that was postponed for a generation, for thirty years, by debt that could no longer be expanded. By 2007 an entire mass of American people were literally exhausted, exhausted physically by all the work; and exhausted psychologically because the family that had held people's lives together had been blown apart because of the destructive consequences that overworking had put on the family.

Women had held the emotional life of families together. When both parents' work moves out of the house and into the workplace, for all kinds of reasons, good and bad, the bottom line is often that the tensions in the family become unmanageable. There's a reason why the sitcom of the 1950s and 1960s was the happy family, the Nelsons, whereas the sitcom of today is the dysfunctional family. So I think that when 2007 comes, the American working class is physically exhausted, psychologically stressed. Let me remind people that we are 5 percent of the world's population; we consume 65 percent of the world's psychotropic drugs, tranquilizers, mood enhancers.

One of the reasons why today's crisis is so severe, long-lasting and defies the efforts of the U.S. government to cope is because it isn't a typical business cycle. This is the culmination of a thirty-year postponement of what it means when 150 years of wage increases comes to an end.

An inherently unstable system, the history of capitalism is punctuated with a series of busts, depressions and recessions. Is this one different? And if so, in what way?

I think this one *is* different. First let me comment on your good point about capitalism being an inherently unstable system. And there's no polite word for that. I sometimes like to make my students giggle by saying to them something like this: If you lived with a roommate as unstable as this economic system, you would have moved out long ago or demanded that your roommate get professional help. We, however, live in a capitalist system and we make neither kind of demand, even though the reasons to do so are pretty much the same. Capitalism is notorious for its upper and downs. We have a whole vocabulary in English to refer to that: booms and busts, recessions and prosperities and depressions and upturns and downturns. You know, the reason people have a lot of words for the same thing is because it's a very important phenomenon in their lives, and they need a diverse vocabulary to articulate it.

You would expect that a population that lives in a capitalist system would know this about its history and would therefore not believe that it was over; that somehow we had managed in some magical way to escape the instability. But the truth of the matter is that over the last thirty to forty years, we have been a society unable and unwilling to think critically about capitalism. And it shows. We thought we weren't going to have any more of these crises like we had, for example, in the 1930s, ten years of depression, or that the Japanese have had, which is twenty years of depression since 1990. It was only wishful thinking to believe that these kinds of things no longer had relevance to our modern life. So we were, of course, unprepared for what we have.

Nothing shows U.S. unpreparedness more than the inability of either President Bush or President Obama to deal with this problem effectively. We are suffering now with the risks and dilemmas of this economy as much as we were last year and the year before and the year before that. This is a sign of a society that hasn't come to terms with capitalism in general.

When I began my work as graduate student getting a Ph.D. in economics, the typical department's curriculum had a course called "The Business Cycle," where students were at least, for a semester, introduced to a history of the ups and downs of capitalism, their causes and what was done to try to cope with them. Nowadays, in 2011, if you do a survey of curricula in graduate programs in economics, you will find the vast majority of schools have no course in the business cycle at all. It was felt that the problems and inherent instability of capitalism had been overcome and mastered.

It was never true. It should have never happened. But it helps explain and illustrate the kind of euphoria people had for thirty years, that we were in a new economic system, that it was a mature capitalism, that we now had all the mechanisms to control the system. The irony is, it left us unprepared to see it coming, although we should have, and it has left a generation of economists unprepared to manage it, which you can see in terms of the inability of the advisers both of President Bush and of President Obama to come up with a reasonable plan to deal with this situation.

So I think the answer is, we have a very severe economic downturn because not only is capitalism always unstable, but this one comes at the end of a thirty-year program of denial, of substituting credit for a working economy that grows and allows people to have higher wages. We never helped our people understand any of this, so now it's like a tsunami has hit us as a nation. And we look really badly equipped as well as unprepared to deal with it.

To what extent do the mainstream media contribute to this lack of understanding as to what has happened?

I don't single them out , but they certainly have contributed. First of all, the mainstream media have not been intellectually alive as critics of the system. I would describe the media much as I would describe my own profession of economics as being more like cheerleaders than like analysts. As a whole, it's been cheering that capitalism is an efficient growth engine that would make everybody happy, that capitalism delivers the goods. The courses, the students, the training, the whole experience of economics as a discipline produced a generation—maybe even two generations—who thought that what economics was about was celebrating capitalism's greatness instead of a balanced assessments of its strengths and weaknesses that might have contributed to a national discussion and better policy.

Capitalism is an institution. It's like your public school

system or your health care delivery system. We as a nation think it's appropriate to question and debate whether our schools and health care system are working adequately, meeting our needs. Why in the world has it been taboo to ask, is the capitalist system, the way we organize the production and distribution of goods and services, working to meet our needs or not?

But it's been made a taboo to ask those kinds of questions. The Cold War and many other things made it impossible to question, let alone criticize, capitalism. Instead of that being a normal exercise of a democratic society evaluating its institutions, it turns out to be an act of disloyalty or something we shouldn't have. It gets squelched and marginalized. The U.S. mass media went right along with that plan and denied the American people a critical sense of its flaws. If the public had been better informed, when the big breakdown happened, as it did in 2007 and 2008, we would have been much better prepared, not so surprised, and in a much better position to cope with it.

There's a certain kind of market fundamentalism. Capitalism is equated with freedom—we're all for freedom, of course—the free market, the free enterprise system. In some respects it's almost taken on a theistic, theological dimension. To question it becomes equivalent to heresy.

In the 1970s, employers were free to stop raising the wages of the mass of their workers. But their exercise of that freedom deprived the mass of Americans of a rising standard of living based on their continually rising productivity. That is, workers after the 1970s were increasingly productive, as they had been before, but now their increasing productivity no longer also provided a better living. Capitalists kept their workers' wages stagnant because they didn't have to continue to share a portion of the fruits of their workers' rising productivity. So the freedom of one part of our population deprived another part of the population of its freedom to prosper from its own work.

Seen in this light, freedom is not a universal good that only has happy news as a result. An honest person says, "Okay, if this group's freedom is given up, what is the impact on the freedoms of others?" If you ask that question, you discover that freedom is a complicated matter: If you enhance the freedom of some, it often involves depriving others of their freedom. To face that would require a much more critical notion of freedom and democracy than the kind of happy, cheerleader mentality we have, in which we imagine, because it saves us from difficult thinking, that enhancing freedom of somebody is always good for everybody else. It isn't.

How do you talk about freedom to the more than 20 million Americans who have no job now? Are they free? They're not free. They've been denied the freedom that comes from having a decent job, and through no fault of their own. Something didn't go wrong with 20 million Americans who suddenly can't get jobs or can't get the jobs they want in a way that they used to. That isn't a problem of individuals, that's a problem of an economic system that isn't delivering the goods.

So I think that you're right, that this debate and discussion of freedom has been like so much in our culture since the 1970s: Very carefully abstracted from the hard economic realities that were unfolding over that time and that were, in fact, depriving huge numbers of our people, a majority, of freedoms that they had enjoyed for a long time before but were no longer available.

One of the salient characteristics about the Great Recession is long-term, chronic unemployment. Is this something that distinguishes this economic crisis from previous ones?

The statistics are startling. The proportion of unemployed that have been without work for more than a year, which is a standard statistic that economists use, is greater than what we have seen in any economic downturn for many years. So there's no question that one of the ways this crisis is more severe than any we've seen since the Great Depression of the 1930s is in the longevity of unemployment.

Other economic downturns like this in the U.S. have had a "recovery" at least for a while. But the reality in the U.S. is, while there has been much discussion of recovery, roughly from the spring of 2009 to the spring of 2011, that recovery didn't affect the vast majority of Americans. We did have a recovery from early 2009 to early 2011, but only for banks, insurance companies, large corporations, and the stock market. Those are important parts of our economy, heaven knows, but they only affect a relative minority of the people. For the vast majority of Americans, there has been no recovery. It's not appropriate to talk about a double dip as if there's a second downturn, because they never had the upturn to make this downturn the second one. If you look at the number of people who lost their job, or the number of people losing their homes through foreclosure, or the number of people whose benefits have been cut—sick days, pensions, and all the rest of it—then the mass of the American people have had a crisis in their lives, economically speaking, for more than four years now.

To talk about recovery to these people, as the mass media did, is cruel. What it does is it makes each individual American, who isn't participating in this recovery, feel as though it's somehow his or her personal fault or failing: *Everybody else is recovering. I'm not.* That's cruel. That inflicts a psychic punishment to people who are not responsible for this crisis in the first place and who should not have been told about a recovery as if it were general when it never was general. That would have helped them to avoid feeling angry and betrayed. Nothing shows the anger and sense of betrayal of the American people more than the political turns in our society over the last few years, whether it's anger in the Tea Party movement or anger that's building elsewhere. And part of the reason for that is the peculiar way we couldn't debate our capitalist system beforehand, we wouldn't prepare ourselves to deal with its ups and downs. We now reap the whirlwind that results from such an incapacity to debate your own economic system and face its problems.

The conventional chronology of the economic crash actually is dating from, I believe, the summer of 2008, when Lehman Brothers went belly up. What happened in 2007 that you identify as having triggered this?

The real shift shows up first in the sector of our economy that has in many ways been the epicenter—the housing industry—the building of homes, the furnishing of homes, the redesign of communities, construction. And that was in an unsustainable boom basically from 2001.

Why do you say it was unsustainable?

Because the boom was based on cheap credit—a key reason we had a boom in housing, in building housing, in construction jobs—and by the way, this affects all parts of American culture. The boom in our housing construction enabled a vast flood of Mexican young men and women to come and work in the home maintenance industries, legal and illegal. The intensification of the immigration problem was a direct derivative of the housing boom. It was created in the aftermath of 2001 because we had a very bad stock market crash early in 2000. That whole period of time from the crash of the market early in 2000 until September 11, 2001 put the American economy in a very bad position, with a major economic recession bearing down on us.

The government's response at that time was to drop interest rates. Over a one-year period, the Federal Reserve reduced interest rates faster and further than had ever happened in U.S. history. It suddenly reduced the cost of borrowing money—that's what it means if you drop interest rates—on an unprecedented scale. If you remember what I mentioned to you before, that we had a twenty-five-year history prior to that of Americans becoming more and more debt-dependent. Then lowering interest rates was like fueling an addiction with more of the drug. In effect, the Federal Reserve said to an American population that was already borrowing too much, Here, borrow even more, and we'll make it cheaper for you.

So Americans did. They started in 2002 and 2003 by using their houses as a kind of cash machine, refinancing their homes, going and borrowing more money against their homes, which the banks were eager to lend to them at very low interest rates. And so you had an artificially driven housing boom. Many people built a new addition on their home. Young people were able to take out huge mortgages at very low interest rates without having to put much down, so houses were built like crazy. There was something of an explosion in building that went on—and here's the answer to your question—until the middle of 2007.

Then it started going down. Suddenly it became clear that many of those people who had borrowed vast amounts of money at low interest rates didn't have the income that would allow them to raise enough money to sustain those debts. They couldn't pay. They couldn't pay off their mortgages. And many middle-class people who had bought a second home because it was so cheap to borrow the money, now couldn't sustain that. They were beginning to lose their jobs. They were beginning to suffer from the cutback of benefits. They were beginning to have medical expenses—all kinds of pressures that made it impossible for them to keep up the payments.

It showed up first in the housing industry, as people were defaulting, beginning to default on their loans to pay for the houses. Houses were beginning to be foreclosed and put back on the market, so that potential buyers were now no longer needing to build a house, to engage a builder to make a house, because there were so many houses being dumped on the market by people who couldn't pay for them. So suddenly the house builders saw their market collapse. That began in the middle of 2007, and it dragged the whole economy down, partly because the whole economy had been built up on this credit bubble fueling the housing industry. So when that stopped, the whole system began to implode. So within one year, by late summer of 2008, it became a wholesale collapse.

The reason for that is important. In the thirty years since the 1970s, as wages were stagnant, the other side of the coin was that productivity kept rising. That is, workers didn't get paid more by their employer, but they kept producing more for the employer, because of the computer that they had to work with, because they were working harder and longer hours, because they had better training, because there were more and better machines. In other words, what we had had before the 1970s continued after the 1970s in terms of worker productivity. American workers are productive and continued to become more so.

Now let's put the two together. If what the employer

pays the worker since the 1970s is flat, doesn't go up, but what the worker gives the employer for every hour of his or her work keeps going up—that's what rising productivity means—then, again, look at what the results are. Basically, it's been the best thirty years that capitalists in this country have ever had because they have been in the wonderful position to get more and more from their workers—rising productivity—without paying them more. Most of our history over the last 30 years is about this, if you think about it.

The business community enjoyed their profits, but they told a completely different story than the one I just did. The story they told was a kind of folklore mythology. That the reasons their profits were so big was because their executives were geniuses. They made capitalists into folk heroes: Lee Iacocca of Chrysler, Jack Welch, the leading executive of GE. They had books written about them as if they were icons of some magical, mystical productivity that accounted for the profits.

Well, let me tell you, as an economist, it's embarrassing to read. I know and every other economist who looks at the numbers knows where the profits came from. They stopped raising their workers' wages, and they kept getting more and more out of them. There it is. No mystery here. They didn't suddenly become genius executives.

Of course, there was method in this madness because if the reason the company's profits were booming was the genius of their top executives, then it becomes reasonable for the top executives to say, "Hey, you should be paying me since I'm so important to these profits." It's in the 1970s that capitalist top executives begin taking home out-of-whack sums of money. And I say out-of-whack because nothing like that happened in Europe, nothing like that happened in Japan. It didn't happen in other capitalisms that weren't experiencing this the way we were. Suddenly the capitalist system begins paying multimillion-dollar bonuses at the end of the year, huge salaries, huge stock options. So there is a reason to tell a story of the genius of an executive, because it became the rationale.

Americans in the last couple years have gotten angry when they've read stories about Goldman Sachs and other capitalist entities dishing out big bonuses to its executives. I'm glad the American people have woken up and are angry. But they're about thirty years late.

It helps us to understand why the last thirty years exhibit yet another problem of our economic system—a widening in the disparity between rich and poor. If the mass of workers have wages that are flat for three decades, whereas all the increases in profitability and productivity accrue to the top, the employers, then the people who become rich—shareholders, top executives, top professional employees—then approximately 5 or 10 percent of the people are getting an enormous boost in income and everybody else is stagnant. Thirty years ago the U.S. was one of the least unequal societies in terms of the disparity between rich and poor. Now we are *the most unequal* of all the advanced industrial countries.

That, by the way, is the root explanation for why this

crisis is lasting so long. We have put the mass of American people in an impossible situation, so they are not spending money. Those that are unemployed obviously cannot, but everybody else is so frightened by the prospect of reduced benefits, an insecure job and depreciating home values that they're holding back. They're paying off their debts. If they can, they're saving a little money. But they are buying less stuff. American corporations are reacting by saying, "Okay, we'll serve the rest of the world. We're more interested in selling abroad, because the American market is exhausted." That's how the mistaken way of developing our country for thirty years is coming back to haunt us now, to perpetuate this crisis, and to make it so difficult for the government to figure a way out.

Income inequality is well documented and is hardly a controversial issue. There's another factor at work here as well, and that's wealth inequality, which is a whole different set of indices.

Yes, although I do think they have a common root. The wealth inequality in the U.S. has basically occurred by an explosion in the value not so much of high income, but in the stock market—all those people who could hold a portion of their wealth in a form that could participate in this boom in profits. The way you hold wealth that can participate in the boom in profits I've just described is if you own shares of stock in the companies enjoying these profits. The vast majority of Americans either have no stocks or a trivial amount of them. The reason the rich have become richer is because they're shareholders. We might like to think about the occasional basketball star who gets a huge salary or the actor or actress who gets one. They're there, but that's not the statistical reality. For that you need to understand that the stock market is the place to be to really participate in the boom of the last thirty years.

Here's another way to put it. Most Americans have no appreciable wealth. That is, they live on their income. They depend on that job and that check. Those Americans in large numbers that have any property have it in one form: Their home. The home, the house, the apartment, the co-op, whatever it is, is the single most important form of wealth that the mass of Americans have. And houses have dropped in value by 25 percent to 35 percent across the U.S. over the last four years of this crisis. That has made the inequality of wealth greater. For those who have significant amounts of stocks, the so-called recovery in the stock market from 2009 to 2011 helped recoup some of their losses. But for those whose only wealth is their home, their main investment is now roughly worth 33 percent less than it was before. Their job is not more secure, their wages have not gone up, the risk of losing their job is greater, their benefits have been reduced, and the only piece of wealth they have has been slashed by a third. Of course, wealth inequality is even more grievous than the income inequality and is a serious problem in terms of getting out of this crisis anytime soon.

The great Canadian singer/songwriter Leonard Cohen has a song where he says:

The poor stay poor, the rich get rich
That's how it goes
Everybody knows.

It's intriguing to me, particularly that last line. I do a lot of public speaking and media work these days. I think everybody knows what's going on. But the taboo against talking about it is similar to the one against talking openly about sex. We kind of all know what that's about, but there's a taboo against talking about it in a straightforward way. We all know that our economic system is broken, is not working, is causing us grief, pain, anxiety, you name it. But there still remains—less than in the past but there still remains—a large amount of taboo about facing this reality, about admitting that it's happening, and that therefore we have to develop some new, different ways of thinking and coping or else this is going to continue. People want to believe that it's going to be over next week.

I know every president says it, but it hasn't been true. And, by the way, every single president since Roosevelt has also held office when the economy turned down. Not as bad as today, and not as bad as the 1930s was, but they've had downturns. And every president comes up, therefore, with a set of policies. And every president makes an announcement of his policies and says, "These policies are not only to get us out of this crisis but, even more important, my fellow Americans, I promise that my policies will prevent future downturns like this." By that standard every president has been a liar, because none have delivered on that promise.

The current crisis has the potential to be a ten- or twenty-year downturn of the sort that Japan has been suffering, particularly if we don't begin to have a long-overdue discussion about why our particular capitalism—no longer works for the majority of people. It either needs to be changed in a significant way or we have to move to some other system that works better. We need to make our economic system work for us in the way that we want our schools, our health system, our transportation system, and our other basic institutions to work for us. The grounds for doing so are not ideological, they're practical.

One of the factors you failed to include in this potpourri of things that have been going on over the last decades has been the decline of the union movement, of organized labor, which acted as a check against the rapacious appetites of some of the capitalist owners. What's happened to the union movement?

You're absolutely right. Your criticism is well taken. I think that my own relative neglect of that part of the story is itself a symptom of what has happened. The trade union movement in the U.S. is now at the end of a fifty-year period of decline. Year after year the number of U.S. workers who are represented by a union, who are in any meaningful sense union members has shrunk, despite all kinds of efforts by the union movement to change that situation.

Think of the statistics today. Seven percent of U.S. workers in the private sector, which is our major sector, are in a union. Ninety-three percent of people working do not have the protection of a union contract or a union organization to make sure they get treated properly, to avoid arbitrary firings, and all the rest.

But the current attacks waged by governors in a number of states—Wisconsin being the most notorious—are focused on public-sector employees. So we not only have a weak trade union movement but one that is under focused assault by politically sustained, coordinated forces across many states. As a result, the prognosis for the trade union movement borders on dismal.

I think it's been very important that the union movement has declined. Let me give you an illustration of why that's the case. In the 1930s, when we had a crisis that was even worse than what we have today, the people of the U.S. elected Franklin Roosevelt and his balanced-budget conservative kind of platform. But after two or three years in office, President Roosevelt radically changed his attitude. He realized, the story goes, that the crisis was severe, that it was resisting the hopes and measures, weak as they were, taken by the government. In other words, he was in a situation quite like Obama's. But he then did something that Obama, at least has not yet done, which is he radically changed his direction.

In 1934 Roosevelt went on the radio and said, in effect, If the private sector either cannot or will not hire tens of millions of Americans who want a job, then there is no alternative but for me as the president to do that. Under his direction the federal government then created and filled 11 million jobs between 1934 and 1940. This was a direct way to use the government to put people back to work: To give them a job, to make them feel like useful citizens, to give them a decent income, to allow them to maintain their mortgage payments so they didn't lose their homes, and to protect the housing market as well.

Why did Roosevelt do it? The story is often that he saw the problem. Yes, but there's more. One of the things that Roosevelt did was to say to the wealthy in America, By the way, you're going to pay for this. I'm going to raise taxes on your companies and I'm going to raise your taxes, rich people. That's where the money is going to come from for me to hire all these unemployed. Wow! Things that today are virtually unthinkable and undoable at a political level were thinkable and doable and actually got done under President Roosevelt's initiatives. Why?

In the middle of the 1930s the U.S. union movement experienced its most dynamic and powerful period of growth it has ever had before or since. It was called the Congress of Industrial Organizations, the CIO, the future partner with the AFL, of the AFL-CIO, which swept across basic industries—steel, auto, rubber, chemical and so on—to organize millions of workers in a very short period of time. Those unions demanded that something be done about unemployment, or else. They demanded that something be done about the suffering of people, or else. And next to them were other organizations that were strong in the 1930s, various socialist parties and the Communist Party. They, too, were mounting demonstrations in the streets involving large numbers of people.

That gave Mr. Roosevelt a card to play that is crucial

for us to understand. When he went to the corporations and the rich, he said to them, I'm going to put people back to work, and they're going to have an income and then they're going to buy your products. You're not hiring them. I'll take care of it. But you're going to pay for it, because you're going to benefit from it. And here's the trump card. If you don't do this with me, behind me are coming the unions, the socialists and the communists, and you're not going to get anywhere so good a deal if they take over. There was enough fear that that might happen—remember, there's also the Soviet Union across the ocean then—that this gave Roosevelt a card which he played and which allowed him to get the rich and the corporations to pay big time compared to what they pay now.

When people today tell you it can't be done, or if you advocate taxing corporations and the rich to give jobs to unemployed people, and people counter that you're talking socialism, communism, no, you're not. You're talking about following a chapter of U.S. history in which a president of this country, facing conditions rather like today, was pushed and enabled by a powerful trade union movement to take a radically different course that helped change the history of this country for the better.

The sad fact today is that we have a weak trade union movement, not a strong one, and the socialists and communists have basically disappeared from our political life. So we don't have the social force that might leverage the president today, whether it's Obama or anyone else, to follow Roosevelt's example.

The militancy of workers in that period was noteworthy. The re-ality and threat of strikes, sit-down strikes, general strikes. There was muscle in the streets. And today, except for a few examples— would you consider the demonstrations in Madison, Wisconsin, and the like equivalent or not?

I don't think they're equivalent. I don't think anyone thinks that yet. But they are very worth focusing on. I think what happened in Wisconsin was dramatic. It showed that within the U.S. is a progressive force of people who are com-mitted to the trade union movement and who do not want workers to be deprived of their rights of collective bargain-ing, etc., who will not sit idly by and watch these long and hard-won gains for working people be erased by a governor. So I think, yes, it's a very important sign in the wind.

I see many such signs around the world. I think Ameri-cans need to pay attention. There were riots recently in London and many other British cities. British people are very angry about the crisis there and the suffering it's in-flicting upon the masses of working people there. In coun-tries like Greece, Portugal, Spain, Italy we've had general strikes, a rising militancy of the working class the likes of which we haven't seen in half a century. It's all about this economic crisis and ineffective government attempts to fully acknowledge the roots of the injustice and what can be done to turn things around. To imagine that the U.S. is somehow going to magically avoid the problems coming here, even as this crisis deepens, is naïve and counter to the history of the world.

My guess is that we're going to be rudely awakened one

day when we see the other side of the coin, when the other shoe drops. We're going to see an American working class whose ideas of what's going on are not only that it's unjust and not only that it's intolerable, but that the solution does not involve pandering more to business than we already have, sort of the Tea Party approach, but is rather a different push from the other side of the political spectrum.

It takes longer in the United States because we don't have the civic pressure coming from trade union, socialist, and communist organizations that they have in Europe. That's why they've been able to mobilize a left alternative anti-austerity program. What we lack here are the organizations we allowed to disappear over the last fifty years that we just discussed. But Americans will be resourceful. The point of view is well represented in this country. People in the U.S. will either resuscitate those old organizations or they will build new ones, because the basic problems in Europe are the same as those that exist here.

Warren Buffet, one of the wealthiest Americans, says, "There's class warfare, all right, but it's my class, the rich class, that's making war, and we're winning." Why isn't there more discussion about class?

I think that's part of the taboo of the last thirty years. We had to believe in America that we don't have classes. I like to point out to my students that the U.S. and the Soviet Union, the two adversaries of the Cold War, had one thing in common. Each side had its government and its intellectuals constantly telling the mass of people that they were a classless society. The leaders of the Soviet Union said it from their perspective, and the leaders of the U.S. said it from theirs. It wasn't true there, and it wasn't true here either. We can't discuss class. It's an explosive issue. Again, it's a little bit like sex: it's one of those things not to be discussed openly even though everyone knows it's a fact of life.

So I think it's one of those horrible lapses of our political and civic culture. When we can't talk about something, all that that does is make that issue even bigger in people's minds, even more powerful, even more influential, even to the point of becoming dangerous, because it's this tabooed thing. It's like a child. "You mustn't ever go in that room" makes that room really interesting. I think we will come to rue the day that we excluded genuine discussions of capitalism and class in the United States.

There is one discussion of class here, and that is the magical, mystical middle class.

Right. I always love this notion of the middle class. Everybody in the U.S., when answering a question, says he or she is in the middle class—very wealthy people, very poor people. They all agree. I think that was just an American way of magically wishing oneself to be part of a society that didn't have the inequalities that are so scary. But we, of course, had them. Now we have them in spades. We can no longer afford to subscribe to the make-believe world in which we're all in the middle. We're not.

The U.S. economy is full of signs that the middle has disappeared. For example, the stores that served the middle—Sears Roebuck and dozens of them like that—they're all gone or disappearing. There is no middle. You don't buy your clothes at Sears Roebuck. You buy them at discount places like Marshalls or TJ Maxx, where they sell stuff real cheap. Or even more, Target or Wal-Mart, the stores for the mass of the people who can't afford any more. Or you're at the other end. You shop in a lovely boutique, in a lovely part of town, and you pay five times what everybody else pays for more or less similar stuff but a different logo or label. It's an economy that's splitting into the haves and the don't-haves, with the think-they-haves in the middle, and that's a shrinking part of our population.

I think another way to get at this is to talk about Warren Buffet's important remark. He at least is the first, the kind of vanguard of the rich class. There are always people among the capitalists who are not trapped in make-believe land, who want to face the reality, because they're afraid of what might happen if they don't. Mr. Buffet is very clear. He says, Look, I did a survey—if you read his whole article—of the twenty-odd people who work in my office as secretaries, clerks and assistants. He said, I pay a lower tax rate on my income, which is thousands of times larger than theirs, than they do. In my office I paid the lowest rate of taxation compared to everyone else. He said, I'm the richest person there. The injustice of it is crazy. The hidden message—and it wasn't much hidden in his statement—was that they're going to get angry about this one day, and I'd be a lot smarter and so would the fellow members of my rich class if we understood that and took steps to deal with it than to put our heads in the sand and wait for that anger to overtake us all.

Let me show you how correct Mr. Buffet is. I'm going to give you two examples. The first comes from the relationship between taxing corporations and taxing individuals. If you go back to the end of World War II, here's the relationship. For every dollar that Washington got from U.S. taxpayers as individuals, it got $1.50 from corporations. That is, the corporate income tax, tax on profits, brought in 50 percent more money to Washington than the total tax on individuals.

What's the relationship today? Well, I'll tell you. In 2011, for every dollar that the federal government gets in revenue from taxing individuals, it now only gets 25 cents from corporations. Corporations have shifted the burden of income tax from their income— profits—on to our income, which is called wages and salaries and so on. That's a tremendous shift. But that's what class warfare means. Corporations have warred against people by pushing the tax on them.

Now my second example, the individual income tax. In the 1950s and 1960s the top income tax bracket of an individual was 91 percent. Here's what that means. For every dollar over the maximum—let's just say roughly $100,000— for every dollar over $100,000 that a rich man or woman got, they had to give Uncle Sam 91 cents and they got to keep 9 cents. Even in the 1970s it was still 70 percent. So every dollar over $100,000 you got in the 1970s, you had to give Uncle Sam 70 cents, you kept 30. What is the rate for the richest U.S. taxpayer today? Thirty-five percent. Think of it: a drop in the tax for the richest Americans from 91 percent to 35 percent. That's a tax cut. Nothing remotely like that has been enjoyed by the vast majority of Americans.

So over the last forty or fifty years, class war waged by capitalists have succeeded to shift the tax burden from their corporations to working people, and from the richest individuals on to the rest of us. So when you're angry at the government and you're angry at the taxes and you're angry at the situation, at least it's important to be well informed rather than to celebrate the middle class and capitalism. The fact of the matter, as Buffet knows, is there's a three-decade-old class warfare and an ever increasing number of Americans are its losing side.

Is this crisis of capitalism systemic?

There's no other way I could possibly imagine describing it. I am surrounded, however, by my fellow economists, and an awful lot of them still don't want to face the systemic nature of this, still want to look for a bad guy. The media join in. If you're one kind of persuasion, you think the bad guys are the bankers, if you're another kind of persuasion, you think the bad guys are the people who took out subprime loans and can't make their payments. You blame the poor; you blame the rich. We're beyond that. Everybody who contributed to this crisis did his or her part. The bankers did what bankers do, the working people did what working people do, each one trying to make it in the capitalist system.

When a system has everybody playing by its rules, more or less, and you get the level of dysfunction we now have, it's time to stop looking for scapegoats and understand that the problem is that the system is what isn't working. The system drives all of its parts—corporations, individuals, banks, a business on Main Street making ladders—to do things that don't work together for the economy as a whole. That's what a systemic crisis means. That's why I stress that there was a situation where workers couldn't pay back their debts, for understandable reasons. Here are the reasons why capitalists stopped raising wages, because that was the system's way for them to function. When everybody is doing their part and the results don't work out its time to change the system.

It's a little bit like calling the repairperson into your home to fix that damn refrigerator that has been on the fritz for a while. After the repairman putters around a while with the motor and with the condenser and with the this and that, he stops and he looks at you and says, "Look, I can fix this. It's going to cost you $50 for me to do this, and $47 for that and $50 for that. But I got to tell you, this refrigerator's had it. And you can pump money in and you can blame the condenser and you can blame the motor, but you've gotten twenty years out of this. It's time to move on and think about a new and different way to manage the refrigeration problems you want to solve in your home."

I think we're at that stage with capitalism as a system, and I think the American people have the Cold War far enough out of our lives, we have gone beyond that, and we're mature enough now to realize that despite everything we've been taught, we've got an economic system that does not work and a political system that will not address its roots or the means to fix it. The problems are systemic. Let's finally have the long-postponed national conversation about capitalism, its strengths and weaknesses, how much it has to be changed or whether, like the failing refrigerator, we need a new system altogether.

What immediate steps would you recommend?

I would focus on two things. One you might call a short-term or an immediate step that ought to be taken and one intermediate step, because I know it will be harder to do.

First, we ought to have a national jobs program. What we need in this country is to put our unemployed people back to work. We ought to stop the plan that has now failed for four and a half years. That's the plan of Mr. Bush and that's the plan of Mr. Obama, namely, to provide incentives, inducements, etc., in the hope that the private sector will use resources to hire people. That's been the mantra, that's been the policy. And that has failed. We have high unemployment now as we did one, two, even three years ago. Therefore, we have a failed arrangement here. It is unconscionable and un-ethical to stay with a policy of proven failure while working people continue to lose their jobs, their health care and their homes.

Two and a half years ago, President Obama had an $800

billion stimulus program that was supposed to put people back to work. Congress passed it, but it didn't solve the problem. Then, in September of 2011, the same President Obama went on television and proposed yet another stimulus, half the size of the one before, even though the situation had gotten worse. You do not need an advanced degree to understand that incentives of various kinds: tax cuts, subsidies, government orders have not and will not lead the private sector to hire more people.

The solution is to do it directly. Do what President Roosevelt did after 1934 and do it properly. Use every dollar of the program you're going to use to hire people. Not to provide orders, some of which will end up in the hands of executives or in the corporation's profits. No, no, no. You want people to go to work? Hire them; pay them a decent salary.

And by the way, employ them to do what? There are many useful things that could be done in this country. Grow the capacity of daycare centers, for example, because we have a very sad condition for daycare, that people really need.

Improve programs for the elderly. Our population is getting older every year, relatively. There should be ways to give old people an important way of contributing to this society, and we ought to do that.

Green our society; improve the ecological relationship with the environment which we've neglected, whether that be insulating homes or building a proper public transportation system that will decrease use of cars, that is such a polluter of our environment. Just as in the 1930s workers hired by the government made great contributions from which our entire society profited, not just the wealthy. They built national parks, advanced conservation projects, constructed levees in flood-prone areas, and so on.

Their work turned out to be useful for generations. So could new work initiated today. It is unconscionable for the U.S. to have tens of millions of people idle who want to work, side by side with one-quarter of our productive capacity also sitting idle. That's based on a government statistic that measures the amount of unused floor space in factories, idle machines and tools gathering rust and dust. Instead of what? Being worked on by able Americans who want and are ready to work, who could produce wealth with those available resources would begin to solve many of our problems. So a jobs program is what ought to exist right away. And it's a page from a playbook that worked for another U.S. president when the nation was in comparable circumstances.

But more important than that, I would stress, is the need to democratize our enterprises. We need to stop an economic system in which all the enterprises that produce the goods and services we depend upon are organized undemocratically. The vast majority of people come to work Monday through Friday, 9:00 a.m. to 5:00 p.m. They arrive and they use their brains and muscles to work with equipment provided by the employer to produce an output, a good or a service. At the end of the day they go home. They take with them their brain and their body, but they leave behind what they've produced, and the employer takes it and sells it and makes as much money as possible.

Who makes all the decisions in this arrangement? A

tiny group of people. In most U.S. corporations, that group is called the board of directors, fifteen to twenty people who decide what to produce, how to produce, where to produce, and what to do with the profits. And who selects these people? The major shareholders. Another tiny group of fifteen to twenty people. They make all the decisions. The vast majority of working people make no decisions. If the company decides to close down here and go somewhere else, what does that mean? It means that a small group of board members and major shareholders are moving the factory from Ohio to Canton, China. Okay. All the people who work in the Ohio plant are going to lose their jobs. All the people in the community who contributed to the success and property of the corporation are now going to suffer ten ways to Sunday. Their children are going to have a harder time in school. You know the story. We permit that decision to be made by a minority. That's capitalism. And we've allowed it as a system to dominate over democracy as a system. The majority of people who have to live with the consequences of a decision ought to participate in making it, but they don't. I think that's one root cause of our problems.

Things could be different. Imagine that from Monday through Thursday you come and do the job the way you always do, but on Friday you come to work, you don't do your usual job. You sit around all day in meetings with the other workers and you make decisions democratically, together. You decide what to produce, how to produce, where to produce, and what to do with the profits.

If that were part of our democracy things would have

turned out very differently over the last thirty years. First, in the 1970s workers' wages would have continued to rise. There was no need to do otherwise, and workers would have decided together to continue to increase their standard of living. As a result, the borrowing frenzy and insurmountable credit card debt could have been avoided for tens of millions of people. Second, would those workers destroy their own jobs by moving production to other countries? Highly unlikely.

Would those workers employ dangerous technologies, ones that pollute the environment? I don't think so because they live there, their children, friends and neighbors all live there. They're not going to want, even if it makes a bit more money, to risk the health of themselves and their families in the way that a board of directors located many miles away might be and has been traditionally quite willing to do.

Would they have used the profits to speculate in dangerous derivatives? I doubt it. Would they have used the extra profits they made in good times to allow some managers to get astronomical salaries while the rest of the people didn't? We all know the answer.

In fact, every part of our economic history over the last thirty years would have been radically different, and I think in much preferred directions, if we had a different way of organizing our enterprises. Not the capitalist system's preferred top-down, undemocratic, hierarchical and bureaucratic way of operating corporations today, but a much more cooperative, collective, community-focused way that is democratic at its core.

For a country that prides itself on its commitment to democracy, there has always been a terrible gap. The most important activity of an adult's life in this country is work. It's what we do five days out of every seven, what we get up in the morning and brush our teeth to be able to do, what we travel to and from for. That's what we're doing most of our adult lives between childhood and death. If democracy belongs anywhere, it belongs in that major portion of our lives. Yet we accept, as if it were given by nature, that we are supposed to enter the threshold of our store, of our factory, of our office, and give up all of our democratic commitments, all of our democratic rights. If at least it delivered us a rising standard of living, it might make sense that people would accept it. But now we have an economic system that imposes an undemocratic way of work and doesn't deliver us a decent economic result either. The time has come to question and debate what has been taboo, at our cost, for thirty years. It's time to challenge capitalism.

Where do you get your politics? Who and what have inspired you?

It's a little bit of everything. I was the child of immigrants, born in Youngstown, Ohio. At the time, my father was pushing a wheelbarrow in the Youngstown Sheet & Tube Company, a famous steel company that no longer exists. He was in that position because he was an immigrant, and his life in Europe—he came from France—didn't count for much when he came here. But I was the first child, so it was important for me and my family to succeed. So I went to Harvard as an undergraduate, and then I went to Stanford and got my master's degree, and I finished my education at Yale, which is where I got my Ph.D. in economics. So by most U.S. standards I'm a bit of a poster boy for elite education. And I'm grateful for the education, and I was trained in conventional economics, the very kind of economics that I have been criticizing in this conversation.

I learned to criticize, in part, from the very economics I was taught, because I was taught by my teachers to ask tough questions. And I learned to turn those questions on the very system I was being taught to revere and I found it wanting. Once I saw that capitalism was producing results I could not justify, it seemed to me that an economic system that couldn't solve this problem, couldn't put the people in the jobs they want, with the equipment they could use to produce the wealth that would make all of us better off, that such a system didn't deserve my unquestioned loyalty. It deserved being questioned.

Once I began to ask the questions, then I discovered, like I think a lot of folks do, that I wasn't the first one, that there have been lots of people who have asked these questions about capitalism and have come to a variety of conclusions—some of whom said it needs to be deeply changed and offered ways to go about changing it. And I found that literature very interesting.

I was influenced by the people who designed and developed the body of modern economics that celebrates capitalism, but on my own I made sure to supplement that education with an exposure to a whole range of critical thinkers.

I don't shy away from saying that the single most developed tradition of critical thought dedicated to the study of capitalism was initiated by Karl Marx. His work was built upon that of many people who preceded him. It does not offer the only set of solution to our problems; it has its own shortcomings and failures. But if you want to think critically about capitalism, sooner or later you are going to have to encounter the theoretical tradition of Marxism, because it is the most developed and draws from contributions made from virtually every country on Earth, from a thousand struggles against business and governments supporting capitalism. It's a repository, a rich resource that ought to be made use of by anyone who wants to have a balanced perspective when it comes to dealing with the real problems.

Your answer triggered one last question. One hears constantly from Democrats and Republicans that the government is like a family, that it must balance its budget. Which on the surface seems very reasonable. We all want to live within our means. Is there anything wrong with that argument?

There are so many things wrong I'm a little overwhelmed as to where to start. First of all, the very people saying it, Republicans and Democrats, are on record for the last fifty years of consistently voting for unbalanced budgets, which have been passed under Republican and Democratic presidents alike, under Republican- and Democratic-controlled Senates and Houses of Representatives alike. So I don't know who it is that is supposed to believe these characters when they give these little homilies about what the government ought to do. But in their actions, in their votes as our representatives, they ignore that.

For example, during the summer of 2011 we witnessed an astonishing political theater in Washington in which Republicans and Democrats yelled at each other in front of the cameras about the need to do something about the debt. But the reality was far different. In the year 2011 the government was scheduled to spend roughly $3 1/2 trillion. It was scheduled to take a total of roughly $2 trillion in taxes. That means it was a budget, which was voted into office by Republicans and Democrats alike the year earlier, that required the government to borrow the difference between what it took in in taxes and what it spent—$1,500 billion.

So what were the Republicans and Democrats debating during the summer of 2011? Here's what they were debating. The Republicans wanted there to be something done about the deficit and began with a very bold plan to cut it by $100 billion. Ryan and Cantor, the leaders in the Congress of the Republican Party, pushed that. Let me remind everyone, the size of the deficit this year is $1,500 billion, and the Republican's drastic proposal was to cut $100 billion. That's nothing, out of $1,500 billion. But then they modified their demands, the Republicans, and came down to $60 billion. The Democrats didn't want to cut that much, so they counter-proposed $30 billion.

They finally, after much yelling at each other and much

invocation of the importance of dealing with the deficit, reached a compromise to cut $38 billion. What was the size of the deficit that year? $1,500 billion. They reached a compromise to cut that by $38 billion. That's silly. That's not dealing with our deficit problem. That is an avoidance of dealing with it. But it was portrayed by the politicians and the media as a grand historical struggle.

The truth of it was, both sides agreed that in this situation of a crisis the government has to help the economy by spending huge amounts of money. Why? Precisely because corporations are not spending that money. They don't have any confidence in the U.S. economy anymore. They're not going to risk hiring workers and buying materials and putting people to work, because they don't think they can sell that stuff, neither here nor abroad, so they're not doing it. So the government has to spend the money that they are not, or else we're in real hot soup.

So the discussion about the deficit is phony. There is no other way to discuss it. It's a way of saying to the American people, We want to deal with the problem in a serious way, the way your family would if it was unable to meet its debts. But what your family faces is a problem they don't think they have. By the way, they do have it. The deficit will cause all kinds of problems in America, not the ones they tell us about, a different set. But they are not credible. They are not dealing with the deficit. Over the last five to ten years, U.S. deficits have gotten steadily worse because both parties vote for them over and over again. And they simply try to cover their tracks in these speeches to Americans about what the government ought to do, but when it comes to their vote, there is no reality and no truth to what they're doing. It's a pretty unpleasant picture, because, if I use harsher terms, it would be words like liars and fakers and cheats.

Need we wait longer to find cause to challenge the system?

2.

Occupy and the Economic Crisis
New York City, November 20, 2011

The debt crisis in Europe, what is it about and how is it affecting the U.S.?

It's a serious crisis, as serious as Europe has had since World War II and the Great Depression, and it is affecting the United States. That's basically because of the very close economic links between the United States and Europe. To illustrate, when the crisis first hit here, particularly with the collapse of the speculations and the new instruments, the credit default swaps, the asset-backed securities, all of that, Europeans were affected because European banks were major investors in the U.S. speculative boom that built up to the crisis. So they collapsed the same way major U.S. banks did. Just like here in the U.S., European banks lost their capacity to repay their investors or even refund the money of the depositors because they had risked too much in speculative instruments that collapsed, and like U.S. banks, they turned to their governments for a handout. The same bankers who had been giving speeches for years about the joys of the free market and the need to keep the government out of the economy ran, each one faster than the other, for government handouts.

So the governments of Europe—from the big ones of France and Germany to the little, poor ones of Portugal and Greece—borrowed huge sums of money to raise the cash to bail out the banks and the larger economic system. What they did in Europe is what they've done here: public government taking on massive new debt to issue what amounts to welfare for the capitalist system. The debt crisis of governments is a direct consequence, A, of the economic crisis brought on by private capitalism on a global scale and, B, by the ability of those banks caught up in that crisis to get the government to borrow the money to bail them and the system out.

So now we come to the next step in this absurd story. Governments of many capitalist economies are now in trouble. They borrowed like crazy, they spent the money to recoup the banks, and now they have to pay interest to all those that they borrowed from. Who do governments borrow from? Bigger banks, insurance companies, large corporations, wealthy individuals, and in some cases other countries. The spectacular irony of today's global capitalism is that the economies of Europe and the United States can't function without loans from the world's number one communist country, The People's Republic of China.

European governments now face the problem of having to pay huge interest payments for all that borrowing they did to bail out their financial and the wider economic damage they caused. They realize that in order to pay that interest, they're going to have to go to the mass of their people and do one of two things: either raise taxes to get the money to pay the interest charges or else cut social programs, cut public employment to free up money to pay off the banks, insurance companies, large corporations, foreign governments, rich people who are the creditors of modern countries in Europe. Either of those two options is political suicide for whatever government or political party is in power. To go to your people in the midst of a crisis and say, "Sorry, but I'm now going to have to tax you or give you fewer social programs," is not going to make anyone politically popular.

So what's to be done? If you do nothing, the very banks you bailed out will say to you, "We're not going to lend you any more money because we're not sure you have the political muscle to make your people pay us the interest we're owed." The banks that only exist because they were bailed out by the government are turning to the government and saying, "We're not going to lend you back the money you gave us. And you're not going to be able to continue unless you stick it to your people in a tax increase or social-program decrease," which is called in Europe "austerity."

The creditors in Europe—the rich people, banks, insurance companies, large corporations—are saying, "You must cut back, you governments, to free up the money to pay the interest you owe us." And the mass of people in the streets are saying, "We're not going to pay taxes to a government that doesn't use it to provide us the services we need but instead gives it to the creditors who are the ones you used our money to bail out." This is a fundamental clash and it's not going to go away.

The collapse of the Papandreou government in Greece changes nothing. The collapse of the Berlusconi government in Italy changes nothing. These are just games of musical chairs at the top. They don't deal with the impasse.

Which is the best way to go? Should European governments impose austerity on their populations or deal with the fact that they mishandled the crisis, that they bailed out entities that are now not only not saying thank you but are actually trying to get you to stick it to the very people upon whom they relied to come out of the crisis they caused. This is a fundamental conflict that is going to be played out in Europe. It may destroy the European Union and it may end the experiment called the Euro. If so, it will be devastating for much of Europe. And the ramifications of that will impact on the U.S. in profound ways, worsening the crisis here, raising unemployment, and disorganizing the global capitalist system as it continues to crumble.

People in Europe and the U.S are in the streets in great numbers. Talk about the very selective use of the terms "austerity" and "belt tightening." Because the people in the streets are saying, "Hey, we didn't cause this crisis. Why do we have to pay for it?"

I think they are exactly right. We had a crisis that the people in the streets did not produce. We had government responses to the crisis that the people in the streets did not support, namely, what we used to call "trickle-down" economics, where what the government does is help all of the people at the top—the banks, the insurance companies, the big corporations—counting on them to then act with that money so it trickles down to benefit everybody else, in the form of jobs and incomes. The trickle down never happened. The recovery program bypassed the people who needed it most who are then told that they'll have to suffer further in the form of belt tightening, austerity, fewer public employees, fewer government services, and Congressional committees figuring out how much to cut Social Security Medicaid. It's an awful story. Society has been destabilized by an acute crisis and bypassed by a recovery program for which it is now being asked to pay. It is intolerable.

In the U.S. there's an elite political class intertwined with a dominant business community that are so hell-bent on making sure they're financially secure that they think they can push the full cost of recovery, whether it succeeds or fails in helping society, on to the average person. Eventually—and this, I think, is what the Occupy movement proves—you're going to provoke the mass of people who have accepted a lot during years of crisis, into saying, "That's it. No more. Enough is enough. We're going to fight back." You destroy the goose that laid your golden egg.

You've written that the Occupy movement "ends capitalism's alibi." What do you mean by that?

Almost since the birth of our nation one slogan has been "Capitalism delivers the goods." Rich people are much better off than average Americans. Yes, there is outrageous disparity and inequality perpetrated by the behavior of the super-rich, with their mansions and all of that. Nonetheless, we've been willing to live with it because we've been convinced over and over that "capitalism delivers the goods."

We are now living through a period when it's clear that American capitalism isn't delivering the goods. Instead of a rising standard of living, there's wage stagnation, decreasing home values, job loss, homelessness, and a political system unwilling to admit that the system no longer serves the interests of the people.

For the mass of people in the U.S., it's one piece of bad news after another. A program of the government you counted on is not going to be available. You thought you could retire after a lifetime of work and get a reasonable Social Security? Well, you're going to have to wait longer, and what you're going to get will be a lot less. You thought you might have a secure medical access program? Well, that's being nibbled at and taken away. In other words, you're not getting from capitalism the rising standard of living that those at the top have been giving themselves for decades.

You used to imagine sending your kids to college? Well, now you either have to forget about it or you have to plan on saddling your children with a load of debt so heavy that when they graduate they'll literally be a prisoner of the economy rather than someone who can flourish in it. You put all that together, and capitalism's support, its alibi, its justification of delivering the *goods* has turned into its opposite. Capitalism now delivers the *bads*.

What Occupy is accomplishing is to fight back against this and against the silence and the taboo of challenging capitalism. People are finally questioning and confronting systemic economic injustice, the recession of democracy, and the alienation, poverty, and instability that have resulted from putting the market, rather than democracy, at the center of our society.

You've said that the Occupy movement is changing the country, and, specifically, talking about a change in New York Times *coverage of economic issues, particularly dealing with the issue of poverty.*

The Occupy movement is changing many things in the United States. One would have to make a long list of the ways it's doing it. For one, it's inspiring college students and young people with the idea that change is really possible. After decades of teaching college students that the only thing for them to do is to strive as individuals to get a good job and look out for number one, we're suddenly seeing a movement driven by some of our brightest young people, saying no, there's a better way, and it's the path to social change that will benefit not just you but all of the others in a collective and community kind of action. Such ideas, articulated in many ways all across the country and around the world, represent a shift in the population.

In the *New York Times* of November 19, 2011, there's a front-page article that begins to talk about new poverty statistics. When you read the article, you learn that these are really not new statistics; these are answers that the U.S. Census Bureau provided to questions from *New York Times* reporters about the real extent of poverty. That is, taking into account the different costs of living, taking into account how much support people get from the government, how much in taxes they have to pay, really working out how much money they have left after all of these things are taken into account, can they live a comfortable life or are they struggling or poor?

The basic conclusion is that one-third of the people in the United States today are poor or nearing poverty. We're talking about over 100 million Americans living in these conditions.

So the next time someone says to me, "Why are these Occupy Wall Street folks protesting?" Well, you have a really clear, simple, straightforward answer. What kind of country is it that would consent to 1 percent of the people living in untold luxury and wild excess of consumption while condemning 100 million of their fellow citizens to a harsh life of austerity, insecurity, with minimal access to health care, education, and the other things that a civilized society ought to give to its people? Of course there should be a movement. That is an outrageous way of organizing this society. And my hat is off to the *New York Times*, whom I criticize often, for at least having the courage to take an idea I think they got from Occupy Wall Street and take it a few steps further and do some of the research Occupy inspires and that the movement is clearly a response to.

That one-third statistic evokes FDR's famous comment, "I see one-third of a nation ill-housed, ill-clad, ill-nourished." Would it be accurate to say that of that 100 million in poverty a disproportionate percentage are people of color?

You would have to look at the numbers. But given everything we know about this society, yes, I think it's safe to say that if you broke it down, the proportion of people of color living in that poverty is greater than their proportion in the population at large. But I think it's even more important to stress that if you have 100 million people in the country that are in this condition, it cuts across all ethnic, all religious, and all regional differences. You're talking about every state in America. If we have 100 million people living in or near the poverty line, it means we have hundreds of thousands, if not millions of people, in every state, large and small, who are in that situation. They are everywhere around us because they are one third of us as a people, black, white, young, old, all genders and political persuasions. So they're not invisible, no matter how much the system tries to deny that poverty can even exist in this country.

Indeed, I sometimes think that the reason the 1 percent smashed down, or tried to, the Occupy movement is because it forces everybody to see what the system would rather not have us see; the movement confronts precisely what they don't really want to believe but know in their heart of hearts is true: The 1 percent have way too much and the rest of us are required to live on way too little. In the history of the human race, that situation, sooner or later, provokes an explosion. And what's frightening the 1 percent is that they know that, too.

In media surveys since the Occupy movement began on September 17, 2011, there has been a marked increase in the term "income inequality."

Absolutely. I was struck, living here in New York City, that for the first few weeks of the protests in Zuccotti Park, the media hardly reported on what was happening. Then, the police began to harass the people. First the pepper spray incident near Union Square then the mass arrest of more than 700 people on the Brooklyn Bridge. Those tactics not only didn't work, they boomeranged. They produced more interest and more sympathy.

Meanwhile, the media have become interested, even inside the same newspaper. The *New York Times*, for example, runs stories that are really quite honest and sympathetic intermixed with stories that are dismissive and denigrating. For example, on November 18, 2011, the *Times* ran a piece by James Stewart in which long quotations about Occupy Wall Street were taken from Michael Prell who is identified as a "strategist" of the Tea Party movement, a strange place to go for expert opinion on Occupy. And the language, the words, the adjectives used in the article went far beyond normal commentary into denunciation. So the *New York*

Times doesn't know which way to go either. But it's already progress that from pretending it wasn't there, they now at least feel the need to have a mixture of stories that are sympathetic as well as hostile. I think we're going to see more and more signs of this movement changing the consciousness of the country.

In 1968, Dr. Martin Luther King was in Memphis, Tennessee, in solidarity with striking sanitation workers. He was planning a Poor People's March in Washington, which was making the Johnson White House very nervous. Of course, he never completed that goal. He was murdered on April 4. What about mobilizing the poor? Is there the possibility of a poor people's movement today?

Yes. I think the evolving organization and the evolving priorities and debates about what ought to be priorities are still at an early stage. I am as impressed as anybody that the Occupy movement this new has already had so much social impact. This is a movement that is working far beyond what anyone could have or did imagine: its widespread impact, the fact that most national polls indicate a clear majority of Americans are sympathetic with this movement despite the hostility of the media, despite the hostility of the police and administrations and the violence perpetrated unjustifiably on them. Despite all that, their message resonates deeply and the movement continues to evolve. So I'm very hesitant to find fault, and I'm not going to.

At this early stage they are already reaching out and

again showing their unusual success. They have chosen first, for all kinds of reasons, to reach out to the organized labor movement. And they have been stunningly successful. One of the earliest acts of Occupy was to march to the headquarters of Verizon, a monster telephone company, to show solidarity with a strike of about 45,000 employees, Communication Workers of America, striking that corporation. They weren't begged to do this, they weren't even asked to do this. They did this as a sign. We care about your struggle. We're going to make your picket lines much larger and much more effective.

Shortly thereafter, they discovered a strike at the center of the 1 percent of America, Sotheby's auction house, a place where you have to go to bid millions of dollars for rare paintings and jewelry. So you know who goes there. There was a strike by the skilled workers who assess and manage the art, who happen to be members of the Teamsters Union. Occupy went and supported them, demonstrated out front, sent people in ties and jackets inside to make the point in the middle of the auction. They did it very effectively.

The result is powerful. U.S. Unions, traditionally very cautious about making common cause with upsurging radical social movements, broke from that tradition and went down there. When the mayor of New York, Mr. Bloomberg first threatened to close the park he made the big mistake of announcing it the night before. At 6:00 a.m. the next morning thousands of trade unionists from around New York, who had been helped by Occupy or had already worked with them, came and ringed the park, arm in arm, and confronted the police, who are also members of a union. The union said to the police, "If you're going to clean these people out, you're going to have to go through your fellow union members, brothers and sisters, standing here." The mayor backed down and canceled his order a mere fifteen minutes before the park was scheduled to be cleared.

So I think we're seeing a movement that understands the need for alliances. It has made the decision to ally with organized labor, and is now reaching out to other constituencies, one of which are movements of the poor. To give you one example, in New York City already we have movements of the poor that have a special relationship with a theological institute. It's called the Union Theological Seminary. There are already lots of close linkages developing between Occupy, Union Theological Seminary and these movements of the poor. So I am thinking that in the months to come you will see public demonstrations of that alliance that is being formed.

Notions of solidarity have long been at the heart of working-class values, epitomized in the axiom, "An injury to one is an injury to all." And you've cited a couple of examples. But there's also a different example. In the fall of 2011, the United Auto Workers and Chrysler signed a contract where new workers are hired at $14 an hour whereas longtime workers earn more than twice that, with benefits.

I think that we are seeing what a great social theorist once called "uneven development." Nothing in our country organizes development to be even. So, for example, yesterday's headline announced that the mayor of Detroit, a city that has suffered perhaps more than any other U.S. city in the last twenty-five years, announced that he's laying off 10 percent of the public employees in order to deal with a budget gap to save $10 million. Ten million dollars is probably what it costs for 10 minutes of military expenditure in Afghanistan. Ten million dollars is a trivial amount of money for a Wall Street top executive to take out of his bonus. We are allowing things to be done with $10 million that are not being used to allow the people of Detroit a decent public employee service, which has already been cut back. It's unconscionable what is being done.

And the same thing goes for Chrysler and Ford. To destroy a union and to destroy a working class by getting the people in the plant to vote for a program that applies to people not yet hired, who are now going to have to suffer a cut of 50 percent, that's austerity. It's a way for these companies to make more money. It divides the working class and it's an assault on all of us. The worker who is paid $14 an hour instead of $28 will not have a lot of money to spend going to a bowling alley or stopping by a restaurant or getting his kids some gifts for their birthdays. That's bad for everybody else in the country except for those corporations who get away with it. And that's the way this country has been working. The Occupy movement is challenging that, but we're going to have to get much stronger before we're in a position to rule that out of order, as it should have been.

In terms of the Social Security fund, if it needs shoring up, currently there's a cap. It's around $107,000. Let's suppose that's your salary, that's your income. That means you're paying the exact same amount as Warren Buffet and Bill Gates, people who earn slightly more than $107,000. Where is the fairness in that?

Not only is there no fairness in that, but we only get taxed for Social Security on our wage and salary income. Income derived from interest earnings and dividends—major revenue streams for the wealthy, but not for the rest of us—do not get taxed. That's one of the ways that the rich avoid paying their fair share. The tax codes have been shaped to advantage and enrich the wealthy to the detriment of the nation as a whole.

So, sure, if you wanted to increase the flow of Social Security, we need to go to where we haven't taxed—the rich. Those who earn over $107,000 a year and/or those who get huge portions of their income from the Social Security-tax-exempt areas of interest, dividends, and so forth.

It's not a coincidence. The rich people and their corporations have been smart. They've used their wealth to do something. They know better than the rest of us that if you have a country with a small number of people that are super-rich and a mass of people that aren't, there's a risk when you have votes and democracy, at least politically, that the mass of people who are disadvantaged will use the political system to correct what the economic system is producing in the way of inequality. So the rich people figured out, "Uh-oh, we'd better make sure we control the political system so it can't be used to tap the wealth we've cornered into our hands."

That's why our congressmen and congresswomen and our senators are dependent on money, because it makes sure they do the bidding of the 1 percent and not the bidding of the 99 percent.

That's what Occupy is targeting as its primary enemy, the thing that it's most urgent to change. It's saying, "We have to bring real democracy, not just voting rituals, back into our system." And there's no way to do that other than separating politics from the unfair and unjust economic system—capitalism.

President Eisenhower's comment about the military-industry complex is fairly well known. Less known is the comment of Seymour Melman, who was a Columbia University professor, who talked about the "permanent war economy." Correct me if I'm wrong, but the weapons industry, which is highly influential in the U.S., is extremely capital-intensive but it actually doesn't provide many jobs. It's not labor-intensive.

There have been plenty of studies that examine how many jobs are actually created by government spending. For example, if the government hires people to do things, obviously, every dollar of government spending like that is job-friendly. That's one of the reasons people like me keep reminding everyone of what Roosevelt did. He spent billions to hire people directly. In simple English, if you want a job program from the government, have the government hire people. That's the best and direct way to do this, but it's not the way the Obama White House has gone about it. Instead, Obama stimulates and provides incentives for the private sector. For four years now, the privately owned businesses have said *thank you very much*. They have taken the incentives and hired virtually nobody. You would have thought, in a society that is halfway rational, that since that didn't work, we would go back to the plan that worked for President Roosevelt: Hire people directly.

But economists have conducted studies analyzing how funds spent on different aspects of our society help job creation. For example, what helps jobs most, a dollar is spent on food stamps for struggling families, a dollar spent on improving college education opportunities or a dollar spent building bombs and drones and land mines?

All the studies indicate that because weapon production is highly automated, taxes spent to buy things like bullets, drones and landmines generate very few jobs. That use of our tax money provides a relatively small number of jobs per dollar of government spending compared to, say, beefing up the food stamp program or helping college students or building more hospitals or, best of all, hiring people to do all the things we need. Compared to other approaches, billions spent on weapons is ineffective at helping generate new jobs.

The weapons industry is perhaps a singular example of how the public subsidizes private corporations.

The weapons industry is unique in a certain way. And that uniqueness is important in America, because the weapons industry is so enormous. Not only does the U.S.

spend billions to research, develop, purchase and maintain a massive arsenal of the most advanced military weapons in the world, but it also markets and sells an enormous amount of weapons to the rest of the world on a regular basis.

Let me explain the economics of this. The U.S. government insists on being the monopolizer of these weapons. In other words, it says to the companies that produce high-tech aircraft, missiles and other secret weapons that it, the U.S., must be the *only* purchaser. That puts weapon-building corporations in a peculiar situation. They must invest staggering sums to develop the capacity to produce these things, and are faced with only one possible buyer for the things they produce. In order for this to work, the government has to guarantee that all the investments will pay off, which it does. Sometimes this is called a "cost-plus" contract; a company submits the cost of whatever it is it did and the government agrees in advance to pay them that money plus 10 percent or whatever it is as a profit.

This creates extraordinary opportunities for profit. Corporations are effectively being removed from any risk, unlike other corporations, that try to estimate the market and make an investment and hope it works. None of that is necessary for military producers, because they are not going to go into the business unless the government guarantees it. The way you guarantee it is by giving them a ton of money.

Who pays for it? We do. The tax-paying citizens of the United States pay for it. U.S. taxes subsidize the producers of military weaponry on a massive scale. Periodically an invoice for a $300 toilet seat gets leaked to the press, but that's just the tip of the iceberg. Even when there isn't phony invoicing, there is a vast government slush fund that funds and profits the business people who make weapons. So when Eisenhower warned of a "military-industrial complex," even he didn't understand how massive and how special and how burdensome on everybody this kind of institution is.

What do you think of the assumption the if the Pentagon cut funding its imperial war machine, dismantled hundreds of its foreign bases, and ended its wars, occupations, and operations in Afghanistan, Iraq, Pakistan and Yemen and Somalia, that if all of that were to stop tomorrow, that money would suddenly find its way into social welfare programs, into education, into health care here in the U.S. Is there any historical evidence for that?

Unfortunately, the historical evidence, at least from recent history, runs the other way. When the Cold War came to an end with the implosion of the Soviet Union in Eastern Europe, there was much talk about a "peace dividend." It never happened. Could it have? Sure. Should there have been a decision to downscale our military to acknowledge that the world had no other military superpower? Of course. But like anything else, it would require a mass movement to force that to happen. There wasn't one, so it didn't happen. So I think Occupy folks have to face the fact that the only way that's going to happen is if they become the powerful social movement that didn't exist in the 1990s. We need that to happen today. The benefits to society would be enormous.

Let me add another point. We've had an enormous

military institution in this country since the end of World War II. As a result, staggering amounts of wealth and influence concentrate wherever military production occurs and wherever big military bases are built. Part of the challenge moving forward will be to organize the dismantling of all this in ways that protect people's jobs and communities. We have to have an orderly way to reorganize production. There's going to have to be a lot of planning to make this happen in a way that is respectful of people's needs rather than some summary shift from A to B, which will leave vast parts of this country bereft. We have to let them know that the rest of us care enough about them so that they do not have to become supporters of a permanent war economy out of the misguided idea that there's no other way to guarantee them a decent job and a decent income. They can get those things, but that would have to be the result of a planned demobilization of the sort we wanted to have at the end of World War II. We wanted to have that again at the end of the Cold War. We can have it, but we have to have the political movement to realize it.

And as we've seen with the bailouts, profits are privatized, and risks and costs are socialized.

It's an amazing process. The government goes in and literally announces, "We're taking the toxic assets off the balance sheets of the banks." Let me translate that into English. The government relieves the bad investments made by capitalists. It's a handout. It's welfare. The only difference between that and the welfare that a struggling family receives is that more money was involved. And what do we say? We say nothing as a nation. We have been forced to believe that this is somehow necessary. And now all we're debating is how big the cuts are the rest of us should take to finance that hustle.

Capitalism has historically been resilient. In previous times up against the ropes, it bounces back. How has it been able to do it? Can it do it now? Or is this economic crisis something seminal in the history of capitalism?

A very wise man who has taught me many things over the years once said, "No system disappears until and unless all of its available means of survival are exhausted." I think that's a very wise summary, not just about capitalism but about all the unjust systems before. I also think that you never know these things in advance. I believe in human wisdom, but I also recognize our limits. We won't know what the last struggle of capitalism will be until we're done with it, until it's over and we can look back and see it clearly. So, yes, capitalism has bounced back from many threats, many crises. The institution of slavery did the same, with the system of enslavers doing everything in their power before being forced to change. That was true of feudalism before it.

I do think we are now at a very profound crisis of capitalism. It is more global than it has ever been before because of the linkages among the different parts. It is more subject to the instant awareness of the mass of people of what's going on. I don't want to overdo it, but things like the Internet and

Facebook and Twitter and the pro-democracy influence of technology are having impact. Ordinary people now make news ands break news with cell phone photos and access to the Internet. It is now possible for activists to publish and distribute photographs of police abuse at protests—pepper spray in New York, tear gas and stun grenades in Oakland— while the events are in the process of unfolding. That is very powerful. The Internet is an end run around the controlled media, at least so far, and that creates opportunities that didn't exist before.

So I think capitalism has very basic challenges. Let's remember, we are now in the second major collapse of capitalism in the past seventy-five years. The last one was the 1930s. The National Bureau of Economic Research, the official agency which monitors and declares recessions and so on, counts between the end of the Great Depression, 1941, and the beginning of this one, 2007, eleven economic downturns. Our capitalist economy is a fundamentally unstable system and is now inflicting its second worst downturn in a century. This a level of instability of our economic system that is going to make a large number of people scratch their heads and say, A system as unstable as this, which keeps visiting upon us these kinds of crisis, is a system that ought to be questioned and challenged.

No one can tell at this stage whether the current challenge, the Occupy movement, is going to mature. But I will tell you this: Any movement from below that can have this kind of growth and social impact in such a short period of time is something to watch.

*You've commented that in Europe, the left parties and the tradi-
tional social democratic parties are facing extinction, that they're
committing suicide.*

In countries like Greece, Spain and elsewhere, socialist
governments that often came to power saying, "We will
never impose austerity on the working class because it's an
outrage," got into office and then proceeded to impose the
austerity they ran against. You have it, for example, in that
iconic socialist dynasty, the Papandreou family, grandfather,
father, and now son, Georgios, who eventually lost his position at the end of last year. The socialist party is committing
political suicide. I don't think it will recover for decades, if
ever, in a country like Greece which has a strong and mili-
tant socialist tradition.

The Socialist Party in Germany, which was once a major
party, is also in serious difficulties. It's a sign of fundamental changes in the socio-economic system, because the old
political meanings are not what they were. The old political loyalties are being destroyed. New political loyalties and
new political parties are being established. For example, in
several European countries new political organizations are
emerging that call themselves anti-capitalist parties. That's
a new development. Even the Socialists didn't dare say that.
Anti-capitalist. But the new ones are in order to underscore
that their programs are for a new system.

I think we're at the early stages in Europe of a new political situation, just as we are in the United States. They're
a little bit further along, because they have more of a tradition and they didn't see the atrophy of their left-wing

organizations over the last fifty years. Their trade unions are stronger than are ours, they have existing and powerful socialist and communist parties in many countries. So they have more networks in place. We are starting more from scratch in this country. That gives them certain strengths, but also weaknesses, just like our having to start from scratch is a weakness, but that also gives us strength. And we'll see how this evolves.

We're seeing also more connections between the United States and European leftists. I did a television interview in Berlin not long ago. All they wanted me to talk about was Occupy Wall Street and what was happening in the other cities of America, what does this movement mean. So I can assure you that the Europeans are tuned into this challenge to U.S. capitalism, which is how they see it, because they think and know that their futures are also wrapped up in how this movement evolves.

There are many currents in the Occupy movement. I was talking to one of the many organizers at Zuccotti Park, and he told me that he was advocating for a better capitalism. His view was that we can do better, we can change the tax code and the rich can pay their fair share of taxes. So there are different currents coursing through this movement.

It could not be otherwise in a movement that's so young, that's just finding its footing, that's gathering those stalwarts who are going to be the core of it. I think you're going to see many, many diverse tendencies here. To make your point even more strongly, I've encountered people who get very nervous when I start talking about capitalism and the problems of capitalism. They tend to be the older folks, to be honest. They come from a tradition of radical thinking in the U.S. that prided itself on never raising that question. They were people who worked in the civil rights movement or in favor of gay marriage or a whole host of issues, where the feeling was not to bring up the question of capitalism out of concern that it doing so might dilute the movement, and upset people who weren't ready for that kind of talk. I understand that. I didn't agree with it, but I understand the perspective. Those people are still with us; they didn't disappear, and their concerns and anxiety about this are still in evidence. The wind is blowing in new directions and the time has finally arrived where it's socially acceptable to question and challenge the systemic failures, injustices and harm caused by capitalism.

The level of economic literacy in the U.S. has been underdeveloped for a long time. I'm finding that half of what I do as I travel around the country is teach economics to people who want to understand this better. As a teacher, the best situation is when your students *want* to learn. I think people are realizing that they have to understand the economics if they want to be part of the debate on how to turn things around. But if you have an underdeveloped literacy, then your economic analysis is going to be all over the place, particularly in times like now, in the middle of a crisis.

Federal Reserve chair Ben Bernanke recently said in Jackson
Hole that the recovery is going to be slow because there are "sig-
nificant drags on the economy." What is he referring to?

Turns of phrase like "drag on the economy" offer a lovely way to avoid dealing with unpleasant realities. Corporations now look at the U.S as a "mature" economy—their term for an economy that isn't growing quickly, like a young one would. And if an economy isn't growing quickly, then it's more difficult for a capitalist to make a lot of money by investing there. Why build up capacity to service a U.S. market isn't growing quickly? It makes no sense. So corporations aren't doing it. They're either deciding to invest elsewhere, where the economies are young and growing—Brazil, Russia, India, China and so on—or they're waiting until the conditions here are better.

What does that mean? Well, it means if your business isn't going to grow, then the only reason to invest would be with a flat-output situation where you can still make some money even if the market isn't growing. This means that if your wage costs come down, if your materials costs come down, in other words, if the economy of the U.S. keeps being depressed, workers are out of work so long they accept lower and lower wages because they're better than no wages, well, then profits might slowly pick up again.

What Bernanke is saying, in other words, is that it's a big drag on our economy when the driving motive to give people jobs is private profit. But he dare not say that. So he uses this language to disguise the fact that in this capitalist system, society is forced to wait for solutions to the devastating problems of unemployment, home foreclosure and every-thing else until private capitalists find a further way to make profit in solving them. Until then new jobs just won't be generated, because we no longer allow the government to hire people directly the way President Roosevelt did.

Estimates are now that private corporations are sitting on roughly $2 trillion of cash, money they have gained through recovery from the government bailouts, and they have made enough profits by cutting workers and increasing productivity. But they're not going to take that money and expand business and hire people, because the U.S. economy, and indeed the world economy right now, is not growing, it's shrinking, with the exception of a few markets and places, which is where they're investing. That's the end of the story. They're sitting there looking at the rest of us and saying, "Until it's profitable for me, I'm not doing anything." The fact that the only reason those people have $2 trillion in cash is because we bailed them out is conveniently forgotten.

Given the multiple environmental crises and the pounding the planet is taking, is it desirable to even perpetrate traditional notions of economic growth? Can you envision some kind of sustainable development, as it's called?

Not under the present system. When decisions are allowed to be made privately, by privately funded investor groups whose reason for being is to prove more profitable than the next one they're competing with, under those circumstances development is going to be guided by what makes money, not by what's socially useful, not by what's ecologically sustainable or by what is good for humanity or the planet as a whole.

If you want to reorganize the world economy, then we need planning on a scale that makes what we talked about earlier in terms of defense demobilization small by comparison. We still have to produce a lot. The majority of people on this planet are very poor, they are not, in fact, able to access food, clothing and shelter in the necessary quantities and qualities to meet minimum standards. We could provide for them. We should provide for them. If we wanted to do that and at the same time move in the direction of ecological sustainability, that would require a massive political commitment and a massive amount of social planning. Only a mass movement committed to those will make that happen. Under the existing capitalist system, we are always going to be in the position of imagining it, wishing it, making lovely proposals that go nowhere because they don't deal with the underlying economic obstacle to moving in that direction.

What about elections as an efficacious way to implement change? I think I can say with confidence that a lot of Americans are fed up with the Democrats and the Republicans and don't see much hope and vote, if they do at all, very reluctantly. What about that whole process about waiting for the great leader to come? Will change come from the bottom, as it has in many social movements?

Here's what I feel safe in saying. The bottom is the only

place from which we can expect change to happen. If the bottom doesn't make it happen, it's not going to come. It was always a mirage to imagine that you could have a political democracy expressed in elections and not also have an economic democracy. It's really simple. If you allow an economic system in which 1 percent of the people have more than half the wealth and the other 99 percent have to share the other half, then the 1 percent are not going to be so stupid as to not realize that one of the ways you secure yourself is to control the political system. And they accomplish that with their money, because that's what they have in abundance. So they use a portion of their money to control the political system, to manipulate what the voter knows, to manipulate the candidates from which the voter chooses, to control all of that. They have therefore been able to make sure that the political process does not, cannot, will not even conceive of, let alone move in the direction of fundamentally altering the system that puts those 1 percent at the top. That's what anyone in the position of 1 percent rich, when the other 99 percent are struggling would do.

If we want political democracy to work beyond the formality of elections, then we have to change the economic system. The basic way to do that is through organizing mass movements that can change the organization of production. We need democracy in the workplace, real worker control of decision-making.

3.

Occupy the Economy

New York City, December 29, 2011

*Talk about unemployment figures and how they are calculated.
The actual number is much higher than the official one.*

The unemployment calculation is a complicated issue
that has been much debated among economists and statisticians in and out of the government for many years. So at any
given time the numbers you hear, particularly those in the
media, simply reflect what is in the minds of the folks who
are in charge of the numbers at that moment, and that may
change from one year to the next. For this reason, it can be
quite difficult to accurately compare this year's unemployment levels to those of ten or twenty years ago because the
way the calculations are made continually change.

So let's begin with the easiest part. Unemployment is
usually given as a percentage of people in the labor force
who are not working. What does it mean to be in the labor
force? Basically, if you're working then you're in the labor

force, but it gets more complicated to take into account all those who are not working. If you answer "No" to the government statistician's question, "Are you working?" the statistician immediately asks a second question, "Are you looking for a job?" You be counted as officially unemployed. If you answer the second question, "No, I'm not looking," then you are not officially considered to be unemployed and you are considered not to be in the labor force at all. The percentage of adults in the U.S. labor force has been falling during the current crisis.

This way of counting means that when people stop looking for work the official unemployment rate goes down. Therefore, officially announced "improvements" in employment levels is not necessarily good news at all. The change may not indicate that people got jobs. It may mean they gave up looking, and that is often worse not just for those individuals and their communities but for the nation's economy as a whole. To understand what is really going on involves closely reading the press releases of the Bureau of Labor Statistics (BLS) in Washington or other government agencies. Few journalists bother to read or reproduce the key data needed to properly evaluate the true unemployment situation. Politicians and public relations folks often pick and improperly use numbers to advance their or their paying clients' interests.

Second, because of these complexities, the Bureau of Labor Statistics, the most important source in Washington for regular numbers, has taken to issuing a whole raft of unemployment numbers, not just one. They actually call them U-1, U-2, U-3 to provide different ways of thinking and looking at these numbers to make sense of economic conditions. That's also an admission of the debates among statisticians.

Most economists tend to use the U-6. It measures three groups of people considered to be unemployed in the sense most of us mean when we talk about it. The first group is the people who say, "I am an adult, I am looking for work, and I don't have a job." That's the unemployed minimally defined. The U-6 number adds two other groups. One group comprises people who had a job, lost it, looked for a while, but are no longer looking. They have been called various names over the years, such as "discouraged" workers, but today they're called "marginalized" workers. The final group also included in the U-6 number consists of people who have a part-time job but say they want, would prefer, and are looking for a full-time job but haven't found one. If you put together the unemployed, the marginalized, and the involuntarily part-time, the current unemployment rate is between 15 and 16 percent, nearly one out of every six persons in the U.S. labor force.

These one out of six people are not earning anything like an adequate income—because they are jobless or only work part-time. One out of six means that most U.S. families have somebody in that situation—mother, father, cousin, uncle, sister-in-law. Then there is the fact that those people have been unemployed or in that inadequate income situation much longer this time than they have in previous downturns. So they have likely now used up any personal savings because they've been out so long. They have thus begun to become burdens on their relatives, the other people in their households, friends and acquaintances. People are getting desperate because of all the challenges that come with living like this. With tens of millions of Americans now out of work, the issue of unemployment in the U.S. has really become a problem for everybody, not just the unemployed.

So it is fair to say that this is the worst experience of unemployment in the U.S. economy since the Great Depression. Young people entering the work force can't find a job. Moreover, most economists expect it to continue like this for years We are therefore talking about something which keeps moving toward becoming as devastating an experience as the Great Depression was, even though we're not at those numbers yet.

What about Unemployment Insurance? Is it adequate? And in terms of its length, is it there for people who are out of work for the whole time that they need it?

Increasingly, because of the length of unemployment, we've had to do two things in the United States. First, in order to cope with the fact that people are unemployed for long periods of time the federal government had to come in and supplement the unemployment insurance that is provided by the different states. By the way, to be unemployed for a long period of time usually means that your job has disappeared. It's not the old days, where things were not good for the employer so he laid you off for a few weeks, a few months, and then called you back. If you don't get called back for a half a year, three-quarters of a year, a year, more than a year—and we now have unemployment compensation extended for ninety-nine weeks; that's basically two years—you're talking about a job for which you will not ever be called back, in all likelihood. You will have lost skills, the job will have changed and the employers will have had to make other accommodations. So we're talking about long-term unemployment.

I think it's fair to say that the government has had to step in by extending unemployment compensation. The government also stepped in by providing other kinds of supports through bills that were passed in the Congress and signed by President Obama. Some of those are finished now. So the actual flow of cash to unemployed people has been reduced over the last year, particularly during 2011, because other parts of the laws that gave the unemployed a little extra money have now run out and have not been renewed.

Unemployment Insurance, which has been extended as a sign of the severity of this economic downturn, is itself becoming a political football. That already happened in 2011, and with the election in November 2012, it risks becoming more and more of a football. That basically means sacrificing the unemployed who risk getting a lot less help when they need it most because the issue of unemployment became a political football.

In terms of comparison with the Great Depression of the 1930s and unemployment figures then, they were much higher as a percentage of the work force, but in terms of millions of people out of work, since the population has grown so much in the last seventy to eighty years, aren't there more people out of work today than in the 1930s?

Yes. Precisely because the population has grown, you have a situation in which more people in the United States suffer. Likewise, more physical output is lost because we're not putting these people to work, more people's lives are disrupted and destroyed. Let me remind folks who read these words that every index I've ever seen of physical illness, mental illness, alcoholism, substance abuse and all the other social ills that afflict individuals and families all get worse with unemployment. If you really wanted to count the costs of unemployment—and we know this from the 1930s—read the novels of Theodore Dreiser and John Steinbeck, the great writers of that experience of depression. They will tell you, as psychologists have since learned, that economic depression usually goes together with personal depression. Countless millions lose self-esteem and confidence, damage their relationships to husbands, wives, girlfriends, boyfriends, children, other relatives and friends. The costs of capitalism's instability—especially when downturns cut so deep and last so long—continue for decades and incur incalculable losses for nearly everyone.

Once again, we need to be clear that we are now living through the second major collapse of capitalism in the last seventy-five years. If we were not so ideologically engineered to defend capitalism, we would have begun challenging its injustices long ago. Yet that is precisely what people in the United States have been afraid to do. We have let ourselves be silenced.

Of new jobs that are being created, most are low-end ones, for example, retail sales, over-the-counter, Wal-Mart greeters, cashiers, bartenders, that kind of thing and a deadly category called temporary services. One can only imagine what that involves. Here for a few hours and gone tomorrow. A recent New York Times editorial puts it plainly: "Indeed, work—once the pathway to a rising standard of living—has become for many a route to downward mobility." One of their writers, Motoko Rich, reported on new research showing that "most people who lost their jobs in recent years now make less and have not maintained their lifestyles, with many experiencing what they describe as drastic— and probably irreversible—declines in income."

Even before this crisis hit in 2007, economic research was showing these phenomena. The way capitalism as a system works is that businesses have the greatest incentive to get rid of the workers to whom they pay the highest wages and salaries. It's just the logic of business. If you're going to replace a worker in the United States with one in another country, or if you're going to replace a worker with a machine, the most advantageous worker to replace is the one to whom you pay the highest salary. To say this another way, this is a peculiar system that peculiarly rewards workers who have successfully raised their wages by means of learning new skills, by means of unionization, and so on. The reward of this system is, if you've been successful in getting a higher wage, business has the greatest possible incentive to get rid of you.

So what we saw, even before the crisis hit, was a long-term trend to replace permanent, unionized, skilled workers with substitutes who cost less money. The biggest example of that is temporary workers employed by temporary labor service agencies (Kelly Girl, Manpower and the like). These profitable temp agencies offer employers two valuable services. The first is a work force to which an employer can avoid paying any benefits. This is because a temp worker does not stay long. Instead of having a long-term employee who expects, because it used to be the norm in America, to get a pension program, a medical care program, vacation days, businesses in the U.S. now use agencies to hire ever more temp workers by the hour, by the day, by the week. The employer signs a contract with a temp agency. The temp agency, in turn, is a new enterprise that offers its workers little or no benefits. It simply tells them: We'll place you for at least a week or a day or a few hours and get you the pay for that. So it becomes a way, between the temp company and the employer, to avoid providing many benefits for workers.

By the way, that's why the statistics show a decreasing number of workers in the U.S. labor force who have benefits like secure pensions, adequate medical care, etc. Long-term employees of a company are being replaced by temporary workers. That process has, of course, been accelerated by the crisis. When companies find their profits squeezed, for all kinds of reasons, starting with their own bad planning to cope with this crisis, switching to temp workers is one of the things they are allowed legally to do, even if there's no fault on the part of the workers. That's how capitalism works. Corporations are allowed to try to solve their problems, whatever their cause, at the expense of their labor forces. Temp agencies have made that very easy. Basically, corporations lay off expensive, longtime workers with accumulated seniority and accumulated benefits and substitute very cheap temporary workers.

The irony is, sometimes when I've made that point in conferences, the answer that comes back to me from representatives of the temp companies is, "We're performing a useful social service." I look at them, "What?" And their answer: Look, if it weren't for us, they would have closed down the factories and the offices and moved to another country, and then the American worker would have nothing. So while we offer a much worse deal than American workers used to have, we're not as bad as it could have been. That's an amazing argument, a testimony to a declining economic situation for millions of working Americans.

It's interesting how the use of language also plays into this. For example, Wal-Mart calls its employees "associates." The word "consultant" is also used sometimes to mask this whole idea of temp workers.

It's an old tradition. Business strategists long ago discovered that one way to substitute for increasing workers' wages, which is what they want and need, is to give workers grandiose titles. So bus drivers become transportation engineers, garbage collectors become refuse managers, and so on. And, yes, Wal-Mart, a pioneer in paying workers next to nothing, giving them few, if any, benefits, is also a leader in giving them nice titles. You are an associate, whatever that means. I'm reminded of my discovery years ago that certain U.S. corporations, particularly banks, like to call an astonishingly large number of middle managers "assistant vice presidents."

Let's talk about the federal minimum wage as a device to keep people out of poverty. Currently—and we've talked about this—nearly 100 million Americans, one-third of the population, is in or near poverty. The federal minimum wage today is $7.25 per hour. That level was reached in 2009, and it's been there ever since. What does that do in terms of alleviating poverty?

The short and sweet answer to that is nothing. It doesn't alleviate it at all. Let me give you an idea. The government calculates the poverty level for a family of four, two adults and two children. If only one adult is working and earning the minimum wage, that family's income will be only 60 percent of the poverty level. In other words, that person and his or her family would be in *extreme* poverty. So any notion that the minimum wage is a mechanism to avoid poverty is simply wrong.

Imagine the same family but this time both parents are working for minimum wage. In that scenario, they would have less than 120 percent of the poverty level in the United

States. Most economists calculate that if you don't get at least 150 percent of the poverty level, your life is desperate. That's because the poverty level itself, like the minimum wage, is set far too low. Most economists say you have to earn 150 percent or more of that to have a minimum life. And that's a minimum life without college education for your children and so on. It's important to note that even if you have a family with two adults working at the minimum wage, they fall significantly below that level.

Since the Second World War, if you take a look at a longer horizon, the minimum wage never earned a worker 100 percent of the poverty level. It's always been kept below that. I believe the highest it got, back in the 1980s, perhaps—I'm not sure of the numbers—was about 90 percent of the poverty level. It's fallen back to 60 percent today, as I said. So, yes, the minimum wage is exactly what it says: It's a minimum threshold that separates a person from being literally unable to survive. But it is not a route out of poverty, and it hasn't been that for at least a half-century.

The number of Americans now holding minimum-wage jobs is?

There's quite a bit of dispute about that, but the rough number most of us use is 3 million.

Several states have mandated a departure from the federal level.

It's an interesting example of how disagreements inside the governments of the U.S. can reveal something. I believe that at the latest count, eight out of the fifty U.S. states have decided that the minimum wage of the federal government, $7.25 per hour, is simply too low. The legislatures and governors of those states have enacted laws requiring minimum wages higher than the federal level. The two states that have been the pioneers for higher minimum wages are Oregon and Washington. And as of January 1, 2012, Washington became the state with the highest minimum wage at $9.04, while Oregon's is $8.80, roughly 25 percent higher than the federal minimum wage. I stress that, because that is a significant increase over $7.25. So it shows that at least some of the states in the U.S. recognize what I'm saying here. The current minimum wage is not only no remedy for poverty. The current low level of the minimum wage guarantees to keep millions of Americans in or very near poverty.

In light of the current economic stress, where municipalities, states, and the federal government are pressed to generate more revenues to cover such things as unemployment insurance and providing basic services, talk about the Tax Code, property taxes, real estate taxes and how they are structured.

This is an immense topic. If Americans actually understood the structure of our taxes, they would not only become angry, they might also find our economic and political systems intolerable because they are the cause of our unjust tax codes. Unfortunately, most Americans know very little about our tax system. So let me try to briefly explain the basics of it here and why it is so poorly understood.

Taxes are levied by the government on a variety of entities that need to be kept separate. Some taxes fall on the incomes earned by individuals and by corporations and other businesses. Taxes fall at different rates on individual incomes in the form of wages and salaries versus individual incomes in the form of dividends, interest, rents and capital gains. Taxes fall at yet other rates on the profits or net incomes of business enterprises. There is continuous struggle over the relative rates at which individual and business incomes are taxed and, at the same time, over the income tax rates of richer versus poorer individuals and larger versus smaller businesses.

In addition to taxing incomes, governments also tax individuals' and businesses' expenditures. We get taxed when we buy goods and services whose prices include a sales tax (e.g., when we buy a shirt or pay for the service to have it cleaned or mended) or an excise tax (e.g., when we fill our car with gas or buy cigarettes), and so forth. Governments can also tax wealth: the property owned by individuals and/or businesses.

Taxation becomes more complicated to understand because different governments tax different things. So, for example, the federal government taxes income. State governments tax income, but particularly also expenditures. And local governments, cities and towns, tax mostly property. So the different levels tend to focus on different things to tax.

All of us pay all or most of these taxes. Thus, some groups' complaint that they are double-taxed is either misinformed about taxation, or, more likely, an argument devised to undo a tax disliked by those groups. Consider, for example, that money is withheld by my employer from my weekly paycheck to pay one income tax to the federal government and another to the state government in which I live. I can spend what's left—my after-income-tax money—but when I buy, say, a shirt, I will often have to also pay a sales tax. If I own my own home and/or car, I will also likely have to pay property taxes on them to the municipality where I live. Thus, an initial stream of income gets paid out to quite a few tax-levying authorities. Every one of us pays multiple taxes almost every day in one way or another.

Let's look at taxes more closely. We may start with property taxes, because they're very, very interesting in the United States. The federal government does not tax your property—your house, car, land, money balance in your bank account, stocks and bonds. Neither do the fifty state governments tax property. The federal and state governments variously tax the income flows from property, but *not the property itself*. In the United States, property is taxed only by local cities, towns and counties.

Here's how it works. Nearly every town and city has an official called a tax assessor. This person's job is to determine the value of each piece of taxable property in the town or city and exactly who owns it. Then the town or city leaders can determine a tax rate that each owner will have to apply to his or her taxable property. Taxable properties typically include automobiles, land, housing structures, business structures and inventories. These are often called "tangible property."

The most interesting and revealing fact about the U.S. local property tax system is that it applies to only some kinds or forms of property, mostly "tangible," and not to others. While land, buildings, automobiles, and so on are subject to taxation, the following other kinds of property are not: stocks, bonds, other sorts of securities, and money. Such kinds of property are often called "intangible." There is no property tax—by any level of government in the U.S.—on such intangible property. Thus, for example, if I have a house worth $200,000 in Yipsidoodle, Mississippi, I have to pay a property tax to the town of Yipsidoodle on that property's land and buildings. If I sell that house for $200,000 and invest that money in the purchase of stocks and bonds, my property-tax bill to Yipsidoodle, Mississippi, drops to zero. There is no taxation: not by Yipsidoodle, nor by the state of the Mississippi, nor by the U.S. government in Washington DC.

What is the significance of taxing land, homes, and cars but not stocks and bonds? The kinds of property owned by average U.S. citizens—if they own any at all—are automobiles and homes. Property taxes fall on such tangible property. In contrast, most rich Americans own much or most of their property in the intangible forms of stocks, bonds, money balances and other securities. Yet those kinds of intangible property are *exempt* from property tax.

We could revolutionize the financial conditions of every American city and town—solve all or most of its tax revenue problems—if the property tax system were simply extended from tangible property to also include intangible property. If you want some quick solutions to our nation's fiscal problems, that would be one. Even on the simple basis of fairness, how can we justify having a property tax system that exempts the intangible property owned mostly by the richest amongst us? What a prime example of the Occupy movement's central point about the economic injustice perpetrated by the 1 percent against the 99 percent.

Going further, the U.S. does not tax the property of religious institutions. Every piece of land upon which a, synagogue, church mosque, Scientologist building or Mormon tabernacle sits is exempted from any property tax. If you live in a town that has lots of religious institutions, it means that lots of the local property is therefore tax exempt. The local community still has to deliver the following to all religious institutions: police services, fire services, public education for their children, road maintenance, health and environmental services, and so on. All the public services performed and provided by the town or city must, by law, be provided to the local religious groups. But because they are tax-exempt, they don't have to pay anything for those public services they receive.

When cities and towns deliver free services to tax-exempt properties, it means the rest of the community—tax-paying land, home, and business owners—must pay extra to deliver those services to those tax-exempt parts of the community that do not pay for the public services they receive. In the U.S., the so-called separation of church and state does not extend to finances. Under the current property tax system, whether or not a person or business participates in a religious institution, all persons and all businesses must pay property taxes to pay for the delivery of free public services to all religious institutions. Those who do subscribe to organized religions are nevertheless required to subsidize the institutions of those who do.

This situation can become extreme if you have, in addition to churches, synagogues, and mosques exempt from property tax in a town, the presence of a big, powerful, rich, private university. For example, the city of New Haven in Connecticut, hosts Yale University, its largest landowner and employer and its richest inhabitant. Yale owns over 200 buildings in New Haven, but pays no property taxes on its educational property, which is about 95 percent of all the property it has. Like religious institutions, educational institutions enjoy property tax exemption. Thus, the rest of the people and businesses of New Haven must pay more in their property tax bills to pay for delivering police, fire, public education, and many other city services to Yale faculty, staff, students, and their families. The individual and business property-tax payers of New Haven subsidize Yale University.

While Yale is widely considered one of the richest universities in the country, its host city is counted by the U.S. Census Bureau as one of the ten poorest cities in the United States. Because of Yale's tax exemption, New Haven, Connecticut, one of the 169 towns that make up the state of Connecticut, has the highest property tax rate of all 169 towns in Connecticut. That is because its poor citizens have to pay higher property taxes to deliver free public services to Yale, that makes no payments for them. That's called Robin Hood in reverse: The poor people of New Haven are subsidizing a university that boasted last year of its tangible property in the billions and its endowment (chiefly stocks and bonds) of nearly $20 billion. The U.S. local property tax system redistributes wealth from the poor to the rich.

The relatively few critics of this system have long argued for extending the property tax to include intangible properties (perhaps exempting individuals' retirement savings up to a certain amount) and also super-rich educational (perhaps exempting the first $50 million of their properties, but not 100 percent of their properties). Just taking such steps in these two area of property tax-exemption could go a long way toward ending the injustice of the local property tax system. Moreover, if U.S. cities and towns could take those steps, they would need much less help from state governments, which in turn would need less help from the federal government. So it would be a boon to the nation's entire tax system.

Now let' look at expenditure taxes. Most of those are called sales taxes. You pay them when you buy something. The criticism of them that ought to be made is that they make no effort to discriminate according to your ability to pay. If Rockefeller goes in and buys a T-shirt, he pays exactly the same tax as you or I do. So clearly there's no effort to discriminate according to ability to pay. An alternative to consider might be a graduated or progressive sales tax that rose in percentage with the price of what was purchased or according to what were mass consumption versus only wealthy people's purchases (e.g. having higher sales tax rates for diamonds, rare paintings and aged wines, while lower sales tax rates would apply to basic clothing, etc.).

The other thing about an expenditure tax is that it has built into it a fundamental inequality. Most Americans, for example, have to spend pretty much everything they earn, because they don't earn enough to be able to save. If you get an income that you have to spend totally, you're going to get taxed twice: first you have to pay an income tax on all the money you get; and then a sales tax on all you have to spend. Compare that to a person who gets a very high income. What that person can do is save some of their income and not spend it. Every dollar saved is a dollar that doesn't have to pay a sales tax because you're not spending it. So, for example, if you can save some money out of your income or you use some of your income to buy stocks and bonds, there are no sales taxes on those uses of your income. No government comes in and says, you ought to pay a tax on holding money or buying a share of stock—the way you must do when you use your income to buy shoes or a kitchen table. Expenditure taxes discriminate in favor of people whose incomes are high enough that they don't have to spend it all on consumable goods and services.

Let me turn finally to income taxes. They are by far the largest tax that people in the U.S. deal with. The federal government basically relies on income taxes and many states levy income taxes too, and there are even a few cities across the U.S., for example, New York City, that has a local, municipal income tax. In other words, New York City residents pay income taxes to New York City, New York state and to the federal government. Most Americans pay only to the federal government or to the federal government and to the state they live in. A few states in the U.S. still do not have any income tax.

Let's look at the income tax. I'm going to focus only on the federal government because that's the major place we pay our income taxes. The first thing to understand is that the income tax is the only national tax that has built into it the notion that those who earn more should pay more. We call that a graduated or progressive income tax. The basic way it works is this: everybody pays the same percentage on the first $10,000 of income, then everybody pays a slightly higher percentage on the next $10,000 or $20,000. The higher the income you get, the higher the percentage on the last portion of it. The federal income tax in the U.S. today peaks at 35 percent, so if you earn above $380,000 then for every dollar earned over that amount, you must pay 35 cents tax to Uncle Sam and keep the other 65 cents for yourself. So at least we see there some effort to tax people according to their ability to pay.

I think that principle is very important. It's been the principle of the income tax now for an entire century. The income tax began around 1910, so here we are, more than 100 years later, and nobody, however conservative, has basically been able to get rid of that. The American people, Republicans and Democrats alike, have endorsed a progressive structure of the income tax.

However, progressivity in the federal government's income tax is quite limited in revealing ways. First, it's interesting that progressivity stops at 35 percent. Why in the world does it stop there? Why doesn't it continue? $50,000 more, you pay 40; $50,000 above that, you pay 48 percent, and so on. Why does it stop at 35 percent? That's, of course, a tremendous benefit to the rich—people who annually earn $500,000, $800,000, $1 million, $2 million, $6 million, $10 million and so on. There are significant numbers of Americans in those categories. Why are they not required to pay higher rates in accordance with their higher incomes and higher abilities to pay? That is a perfectly reasonable, logical question for a tax system that is progressive but stops being progressive at a relatively low level of income and a relatively low tax rate.

Examining other points in American history helps drive this point home. For example, in the 1950s and 1960s, the top income-tax rate that the highest income-tax payers had to pay was 91 percent. What that means is that everyone in the U.S. who during the 1950s and 1960s earned over whatever the top bracket was—say, $70,000 or $60,000—had to pay Uncle Sam 91 cents of every one dollar they earned over that mark. I'm not describing the Soviet Union or China or Cuba or places like that. I'm also not describing the United States at the time of the Civil War or the Great Depression, I'm describing the United States of recent times that many people today personally lived through and remember.

Something happened between the 1950s and today which can only be described as a mammoth tax break, giveaway, to the richest Americans. Their top bracket went from 91 percent to 35 percent, and as Mitt Romney's recent tax disclosure reveals, people who earn $45 million a year can get it down to 15 percent, because the system has been revised to serve the rich. So there's no way out of the conclusion that over the last forty to fifty years the greatest beneficiaries of tax cuts in the United States were the richest Americans. Part of the reason the gap between rich and poor has become so extreme in the U.S. is precisely because of the success of the rich in buying the political influence needed to reduce their tax burdens so dramatically.

But that's not all. Alongside the taxes on individuals, let's remember that the federal income tax also falls on corporations. And they have also been busy shifting the burden of taxes off of themselves. The way I summarize that is with a simple statistic. In the 1940s, at the end of the Second World War, for every dollar the federal government got from individuals it got about $1.50 in income taxes from the profits of corporations. In 2010 the same number reads as follows: For every dollar the federal government gets from individual income taxes, it gets 25 cents from corporate income taxes. In other words, corporations have reversed the burden of taxes drastically from themselves to individuals.

Over the last half-century or so, corporations shifted much of the burden of taxes onto individuals, and rich individuals shifted the burden of their taxes onto everyone else. That is a capsule summary of the economic history of federal taxation over recent decades, and part of the force that has driven us into the crisis we are in today.

One solution, therefore, to the tax problems of the federal government not having enough money to maintain a

Let me address the big issue here. Years ago, the Internal Revenue Service told Americans to use the Tax Code and use every gimmick there that might conceivably lower your tax bill. But average Americans lack the expertise and the access to the legalese language. For most Americans, it does not pay to hire a skilled tax accountant or lawyer to do that work for you since it would cost more than such a person could save you in taxes. After all, the IRS gives average Americans the option of taking a general exemption. But the situation differs for corporations and rich people. They often earn more than enough to make it very worthwhile to hire a professional tax accountant because that person can make sure every gimmick is used to lower the rich client's taxes. Corporations and the rich have the resources to influence tax laws made in Congress and tax rules made in the IRS. Then they also use their resources to hire the best experts to take maximum advantage of the laws and rules.

Classic gimmicks include claims that, as an expense of doing business, you needed $300 per person lunches, travel to resorts where you "confer" with real or "potential" clients, and so on. Business expenses like that can be deducted from the revenues of your business, thereby reducing the net revenue subject to taxes. In this way—using rules and procedures to support such claims with an accountant's careful paperwork—you lower your taxes. The rules make that a much less attractive or beneficial process for an average person buying a sandwich for lunch and taking the family for a week's vacation at the lake. In such ways the system is structured to favor the corporations and the rich. And, of course, the more they reduce their taxes, the more the government must tax the middle and lower income people to offset the tax obligations that corporations and the rich escape.

One of my favorite tax-dodge examples involves the charitable deduction. You can give something you own to a charity of some sort and you can deduct the market price of what you gave them from your own income and thereby reduce your income tax. This has led to some creative manipulation among wealthy institutions and wealthy people. For example, suppose you are wealthy enough to have a very expensive painting by Pablo Picasso hanging in your living room. You are also earning so much money that you face big tax bills unless you can reduce your taxable income by finding some legitimate expenses you can use to reduce your taxable income way below your actual income. You need what are called tax deductions. Suppose Mitt Romney owns a Picasso sketch in one of his houses worth $1 million. According to tax rules, he can donate it to a university like Harvard. Like other such institutions, Harvard may be agreeable to become the painting's legal owner, taking it with stipulations that benefit Romney. For example, Romney might give Harvard the painting in 2012, which gives him a $1 million deduction on this year's taxes. He subtracts the $1 million contribution to Harvard from his 2012 income and that leaves him with that much less taxable income this year.

But that's only the beginning. Now step two. Harvard, to whom the painting was given, has the legal right to lend it back to Romney. Harvard might lend it Mitt Romney for the rest of his life. Therefore, the art never leaves Romney's possession, This is all done on paper. It stays right in his biggest house, and it will stay there for the next twenty years, however long he lives. And then when he finally dies, then it will go to Harvard. Harvard is happy because it will eventually get it and it costs them nothing. Mitt Romney is happy because now, many years before he dies, he gets the full value of that charitable deduction and he gets to keep and enjoy the art his entire life. The possibility of using the Tax Code in such ways was the work of clever tax accountants and lawyers hired by multi-millionaires like Mitt Romney. Eventually they get written into the code and become legal ways for the rich to get their way.

In literally hundreds or even thousands of ways, great and small, corporations and rich individuals (mostly directly dependent on corporations) reduce their taxes and shift the tax burden onto the rest of us. So gross has this process become that last year Warren Buffet, one of the richest men on Earth, explained that he pays a lower percentage of taxes on income of billions than the percentage of their income paid by the secretaries in his office.

Grover Norquist, a Washington lobbyist and operative, has been almost single-handedly successful in demonizing taxation. He's also managed to change the actual vocabulary. For example, the estate tax is now called the death tax. When you tell that to an average person who is going to die, they'll probably think, I don't want to have a tax when I die. But that's not what this is about.

112

It's another clever use of language. Part of what needs to be done is to frame language that represents the interests of the majority of people in the United States. For example, we ought to call the property tax a privilege tax. If we called it a privilege tax, everybody would wonder, whose privilege, and then we would explain to them the privilege of all the people who don't pay property tax, whether they're rich universities or folks with stock and bond portfolios and so on.

I think another example that might be interesting to people is Social Security. It's a very big part of what the government has to do now—help Americans who have put in a whole lifetime's worth of work and taxes. Having had money withheld by the government for their entire working life, people retire at age 65. Social Security then provides them with a pension of sorts. The pension is very modest, it does not provide very much money to people. But it's a lot better than getting nothing. And people are kind of grateful in America. It's a very popular program, and always has been, to provide some help not only for the people who reach age 65 but, also for their children, who therefore don't have as big a burden taking care of their parents as they would otherwise have. So it really doesn't just benefit the older folks; it benefits everybody in the society.

An important key to understanding the false claim that the Social Security system is in financial trouble, cannot pay its way and will collapse, is to understand that we do not have a progressive system. Under the law, Social Security taxes are paid on roughly the first $107,000 of any individual's income. Half is paid by the employer and half by the em-

wealthy enough, you will get a memo from your highly paid tax accountant at least once or twice a year updating you on the latest significant changes in the code and how your situation might gain advantages from exploiting them. A clever tax accountant will then work out—perhaps with legal counsel—a plan to change and move assets in your portfolio and elements of your income streams to lower your total tax bill and so on. Most Americans have neither the incentives nor the resources to take comparable steps with their modest incomes and even likely more modest property.

Meanwhile, corporations and the rich are forever looking for new tax breaks and paying lobbyists to do the work in Washington or the state house of a state to get Tax Codes adjusted, regulations shifted, new laws passed. That's why so many particular groups of companies and rich individuals have acquired what we've come to call tax loopholes—minute details slipped into a bill at the last stages of becoming law or into a regulation as it reaches completion. Nobody usually pays much attention, because it's such a little deal that only these sugar farms or those oil drillers or those trucking firms, etc. will gain advantages from. But they will save hundreds of millions of tax dollars or be able to expand their businesses or ignore certain inconvenient rules. It often pays off to hire high-cost lobbyists for years in order to win such loopholes. Once again, what loopholes save in taxes for those who paid for them will be taxes that the rest of us without loopholes will likely have to pay. That's class war.

Lotteries, now run by most states are, you say, disguised forms of taxation. Explain what you mean.

Over the last several decades the U.S. tax system has faced a revolt, understandably, by the middle- and lower-income people. We have already discussed how they came to pay ever more of the taxes that corporations and the rich found ways to escape. It's not surprising that Americans, in general, are angry about taxes and want the wealthy to pay a more equitable share.

This has left politicians and the state in deepening difficulty. How are you going to deliver all the government services, partly to the rich and the corporations and partly to the general public, that they want (public education, road maintenance, police and fire services and so on) if low rates and loopholes and angry average taxpayers deny you the needed revenues? One solution that political leaders increasingly turn to is public gambling on lotteries and animal races. Essentially, the politicians found a way to tax people without calling it a "tax." Instead, the government runs a gambling business; it is "the house" that always structures the lotteries and races so as to yield the house/government net revenue. It's a politicians dream—getting steady money out of the mass of people without offending them, without appearing to be taxing them, but doing exactly that.

Here's how it works. The government establishes a lottery and publicly offers people the chance to buy lottery tickets. It collects their money and gives a huge payout to a tiny number of winners. The rest, the vast majority of ticket buyers only get to experience the fantasy of winning and deciding what to do with all that money. The many state governments that have instituted lotteries take in more money than they pay out and use the difference to help fund public services. By selling the masses pure fantasy—an imaginary escape from a declining economy—a small substitute for taxation is being expanded.

But there are real costs to lotteries and gambling on races that tend to be downplayed when desperate politicians endorse them for cash-strapped governments. During the years I lived in Connecticut, I had occasion to look at maps showing where lottery tickets were sold most across the state. Those maps showed that the lower the average income in an area of the state, the more lottery tickets were sold there. It turns out that lotteries are regressive forms of taxation—taking more, in percentage terms, from the poor than from the middle and the rich.

A term that is repeated over and over again is "the market." But it seems to have some kind of mystical force behind it, almost like a phantom. We hear about the market gaining or losing confidence as if it were a person.

In our culture the concept of the market is akin to religion. In fact, for many people the fantasy that their life is shaped by a market is a substitute for thinking that it was shaped by a deity, or else the market itself is understood as a deity. That is a long cultivated mythology that runs very deep in the U.S. and Great Britain, less so in the rest of Europe, and that has been disputed by thinking people for a long, long time. If you go back to Plato and Aristotle, you will discover that both of them wrote long essays about the destructive nature of markets and how they undermined social institutions and community. Both of them argued that.

A market is a way for people to distribute resources and goods. That's all it is. The human race for most of its history has not used markets to do that. When I say distribute resources, I mean land. Who's going to get what piece of land to cultivate? That's a big issue. You have to distribute the land somehow among the people. Through most of human history the land was not understood to be something that individuals would ever own as private property. The land was understood to be a gift of Nature, the Great Spirit, God, a resource that is part of Earth, like we are. Through most of human history it would have been thought of as absurd, outrageous, blasphemous to take the land, which human beings didn't put there, and give it to one or another of them. Indeed, in the Middle Ages, the Roman Catholic Church said it was a sin to treat land as private property, something you could buy and sell, because it was a sin against God. God put the land there. It's arrogant and blasphemous of individuals to take it and likewise to buy and sell it in markets as if it were theirs.

In some indigenous traditions a tribe would distribute land among its people, not as private property, but to be cultivated and farmed. In medieval times the lord of a manor did that. So there is a long and diverse history of distributing resources in non-market ways.

The same applies to products of labor, outputs of goods

and services. In many traditional indigenous societies elders would meet to parcel out a harvest to families according to what they thought was needed, fair and reasonable. These are all ways of distributing resources and goods that do not use a market that is a relatively modern institution for distributing both resources and products.

How long have markets been the primary mechanism, two hundred years?

Markets have been major social mechanisms of distribution for two hundred to three hundred years. They existed before that, but they weren't the dominant way that communities and societies distributed most things. And let me be clear. Even in today's world, many goods and services are distributed in non-market ways. The best examples I have are all the goods and services produced inside households. Consider a typical Thanksgiving dinner. You've all had turkey made by mama and you've sat around and enjoyed a lovely Thanksgiving dinner. And now we're done at the end of the meal, and Mama says to you, "Oh, darling, would you please clear the plates and take the garbage outside so we can enjoy the rest of the evening." And you, having just been taught a lot about markets, say, "Yes, Mama, of course. I will perform this service for everyone in the room, as long as each person gives me a dollar." At that point your father reaches across the table and smacks you and begins a heavy lecture. "That's outrageous what you just did," Papa says, "because this is a family. We love each other, and we do things for each other out of affection, out of love, out of respect. It is outrageous for you to demand money for that." Wow. Let me translate into economic language what Papa just said. A market is what Papa does not have and does not want in the house. He wants goods and services produced by household members distributed according to criteria of love, respect, need and desire. Mama didn't charge family members for pieces of the turkey she bought, cleaned, cooked and served. You are not allowed to establish a market inside the house for the cleaning service you were asked to perform. The market is banned, papa explains, because a market would destroy the love amongst us, would be incompatible with the family relationships.

When I tell this story to students when I teach, I usually stop at this point to lean across the podium and say to my class, "Here's a thought. If a market is incompatible with love inside the household, maybe it is outside, too. Maybe it isn't an institution we want. To revere the market uncritically, as some holy or perfect institution, is to be dishonest about our own lives, to lack the courage Papa showed at the Thanksgiving dinner. We don't permit markets in many other distributions of goods and services besides the household. For example, societies have long held markets in sexual services to be immoral, intolerable, etc., and often banned them altogether."

Having said that, let me turn now to the larger society, where we do use markets. Markets are certainly one way of distributing goods and services. But they're not the only way, and they're not ethically, morally or economically all that desirable. Think of it this way. A market means human beings like you and me every day are put into the following situation. We enter a store, a factory, an office, and we try to do something that, even if we're unconscious of it, doesn't make it any less important in our lives. We are best served if we give up as little money as possible to get the best quality and/or greatest quantity as possible. The other side of this transaction has the same motivation in reverse. We basically find ourselves in an adversarial relationship with everyone we engage in market exchanges. When we can get a little more coffee in the cup, we try to. When we can get away with not paying for something, a lot of us do it. Not a few of us find these market relationships so unpleasant that we shy away from them, insist on violating their norms, or pretend they do not exist (or become unconscious of them). And we produce all kinds of inefficiencies, problems and injustices by market mechanisms of distributing. It has a lot of problems associated with it, number one.

Number two, a market is, if you think about it, a very inegalitarian way of distributing goods, because everything happens according to people's capacity to pay. So, for example, if there is a shortage of milk and I only have $10 in my pocket, I can offer up to $10 for the milk because I need it for my child, but standing next to me is another person who has $50 in his pocket, that person can offer more for the milk and will get it because he can pay more. A market distributes goods and services according to people's ability to pay. It does not inquire as to whether the people who have a greater ability to pay got it by working hard, by stealing it, by inheriting it, or any other way. So it's important to remember that markets are a very particular way of distributing goods and services and not one that we ought to think of as all that desirable.

Indeed, I can give you a concrete example of that. During World War II, it was felt in the U.S. that we as a nation had a primary interest in coming out of that war as a winner rather than as a loser. In order to win that war, lots of resources were needed to sustain our Army, our Air Force, our Navy. We did not, therefore, want resources needed to pursue the war to be used instead by people who could afford to buy those resources because they had a lot of money. So how did the government handle that? Basically, it told rich people, "You have a lot of money, which normally in a market would allow you to get whatever you want and deny it to people with less money. We don't want that to happen, not because of concern for poor people but concern because we need those resources to win the war. But we also have another concern: if we allow some resources to go for the war and the remaining resources to be given to those who have the most buying power, the mass of people who then get denied those remaining resources may get very angry. And we can't afford a social division between those the market serves and those the market screws, because that division will make it harder to win the war."

So what did the government do? It superseded the market. It said, "Markets don't work in this situation." And it issued something called ration cards to Americans. If you wanted a quart of milk, if you wanted a pound of sugar, if you wanted a gallon of gas for your car, and if you wanted a whole lot of other things, you had to have more than just the money to pay for it. You also had to have a ration card, which was issued by the government to people not according to how much money they had but according to their needs as human beings. If you had a family with 10 children, you got a lot more ration cards than if you had a family with three children.

This wonderful example illustrates that at a time of urgent national need we didn't want to rely on a market, we didn't allow the market, because the market gave us results that were considered socially unwanted, socially ineffective, dangerous for the survival of the society. I would argue that that's always true; it's not just true in a war. A market distributes goods and services to those most able to pay. I don't think that's useful, I don't think that's necessary. I think that's fundamentally immoral. And I think most Americans would agree if they could see that that's what a market is.

Finally, capitalists and other advocates of markets argue that even if it isn't all that morally attractive to distribute goods according to people's ability to pay without regard for how they got that ability to pay or for their needs as fellow citizens, at least, they argue, it's efficient. It's a wonderfully efficient way to allocate resources; it keeps the economy humming. My answer to them is, hello, what planet do you live on? Here we are in 2012, in the fifth year of a fundamental economic crisis where this charming market system, which we are told is so efficient, has produced 20 to 25 million people out of work, 30 percent of our industrial capacity unutilized, sitting there rotting, and vast amounts of wealth lost that these unemployed people could have produced with those tools and equipment. Then we are told the market system is efficient? Wow.

If you're halfway there by understanding it's not ethical, I have news for you. It's not very efficient either. It is only maintained by those—and they are the minority—who benefit from the market. Those, again, are the richest amongst us, because in a market system the goods and services go to them and not to the rest of us. That they love markets, I understand. That the average American is loyal to markets, that's a testimony to generations of social engineering and PR done by that minority.

Pensions. You write that the U.S. pension systems for workers are now widespread disasters.

The first problem is that we have two kinds of pensions in the United States, public and private. The public pension system is the Social Security system. The average amount that people collect from Social Security is approximately $12,000 per year. Clearly, it is very difficult for a person of any age to live on $12,000 per year. So the public pension, if you even get it—and not all people in the U.S. are eligible for it—isn't going to sustain you. That means, if you're going to have a reasonable retirement period after you've given thirty, forty, fifty years of active labor to this society, if you want your retirement years to be a source of satisfaction to you and not to be a burden on your children and your friends, you're going to need to have a private pension on top of the small, meager public pension.

An increasing number of Americans have no private pension. That's because employers, who used to provide pensions as a kind of benefit, alongside a medical plan and a few days of vacation a year and so on, have been cutting back on pensions. So at this point a majority of Americans either get no private pension or a very small, meager one. And the numbers of people eligible for pensions from their private employer has been declining for quite some time now, and particularly during the current crisis.

But here's the worst part. Even more dramatic than the change in the number of people covered by pensions or in the size of those pensions has been a change in the kind of private pensions that Americans qualify for. It used to be that the pension provided by an employer was overwhelmingly of the kind described as a "defined benefit" pension. What that means is the pension you got was something promised to you, a certain number of dollars per week or per month, that would be adequate to live in a reasonable way, often with a cost-of-living clause added to it so that if prices rose, so did your pension. It was an obligation of your employer to see to it that you had a reasonable support in your old age.

Those kinds of pensions are largely disappearing. They've not just been reduced; they're on the way out. They're being replaced by something called a "defined contribution" pension. In these pensions, what happens is the employer doesn't commit to provide you with a reasonable retirement life at all. All the employer now commits to do is to put aside a certain amount of money into a fund, often a fund that you yourself can "manage," as if you knew how to play the stock market, which most people don't. The result is, it's kind of a crapshoot. You're now having money put aside by your employer, if you're lucky enough to have a private pension at all, but you depend on the ups and downs of the stock market to determine how much money will be available for you when you retire. And it will be a certain amount of money, and who knows how adequate it will be in terms of inflation, which may eat away at it, in terms of your living a long time, so you may run out of it. So there are all kinds of problems with a defined-contribution pension. To make a long story short, corporations don't do that to help you. They did that to help themselves, to cheapen the cost of employees' pensions, and therefore to put employees' pension benefits at risk.

Corporations have also systematically underfunded their pensions. This is worth understanding. A corporation is supposed to put aside enough money so that you can be reasonably sustained if there's a pension program in effect where you work. But companies have all kinds of ways of underfunding, not putting aside enough money. That has been recognized for a long time. So that there's a government agency whose job it is to provide insurance for—in effect, to guarantee—pension funds. It's a backstop, when pensions are not sufficiently funded by the private employer so that people are not screwed because of the misbehavior of their employer. You can see how dangerous this gets, because you can work at a place for thirty or forty years, then you get ready to retire, and the company announces it's underfunded its pension. What do you do? Or worse still, the company goes out of business, declares bankruptcy, and then you discover that they don't have much in their pension fund as they go bankrupt. What are you going to do? There is now a government agency that's supposed to step in.

But it turns out that that government agency is on the hook for what could potentially be many, many billions of dollars for unfunded or underfunded pensions both public and private. The problem is that the only way the government could actually make good on the guarantees that it has given pensions through its little insurance program is by raising everybody's taxes to get the money. Can you imagine the outcry across America with our regressive tax structure imposing further burdens on the mass of people to make up for the employers who didn't fund their pensions?

Wasn't part of the logic of setting up pensions by corporations to reduce the cost of employee turnover? You wanted to have that person in the job for many, many years, because if they left, the retraining and all of that would cost much more money. In return for providing the pensions the corporations offered less in wage increases, and the unions, when they were negotiating, went along with this.

Yes. That's why it is dishonest for capitalists and defenders of corporations to argue that this is some sort of gift to the workers, some sort of largesse on the part of the employer. Pensions were always fought for by workers. They were not offered by corporations. When workers finally won pensions it was part of the negotiations between unions and employers in which the medical care program, the pension, and the wages were dealt with together. What you didn't get in the way of wages you got in the way of a pension. Or to say the same thing another way, a worker who won a pension from his employer had to pay for it by giving up a wage increase he could otherwise have gotten. So in a sense, to not pay the pension is to have screwed the worker out of wages to get a pension, and then to screw him out of the pension on top of it.

There is another dimension of this. We have a high unemployment level now in the United States, and more skilled working people are coming out of our high schools and colleges than employers want to hire. This has led corporations to think, "Well, we don't need to retain workers. We have a vast pool of skilled workers to choose from, so we don't need to offer a pension." So in a sense they're taking advantage of the dysfunctional market economy we have to deprive workers of the kinds of pensions that they used to have.

In a decent society it wouldn't be up to an employer's honesty or dishonesty to say that we have an obligation to people who have gotten an education, worked hard all their lives, given thirty, forty, or more years of hard work. They should be given a decent time to retire, to help take care of their grandkids, to do what they want after having contributed that much, without making it conditional, dangerous, insufficient. That is a grotesque way of dishonoring older people, who deserve the respect and a decent life, without being a burden on their children. What they paid for all their working lives ought to be provided. The state ought to do it. It ought to be a matter of right, like going into a public park with your children on a sunny afternoon is a public right, and not limited to the whims and the honesty of an employer, especially having seen how many of them are not up to the task.

Reforms. Talk about the intrinsic limits of reforms when the economic problems are systemic.

As we discussed before, the 1930s was the last time we had a terrible economic breakdown of capitalism. As a result of that, masses of people became very critical of the economic system because it was hurting them so badly. We had a powerful trade union movement, we had strong socialist and communist parties, and they put a lot of pressure on the government to do something. The government responded by enacting reforms and these offer a concrete example of what can and cannot be done.

The first big reform was to create a the Social Security system. We never had that before and it has since become a basic feature of American life. In the depths of the Depression, the mass of people demanded help for old folks, retired workers, and the government provided it.

The second major reform was to create Unemployment Insurance. The idea driving its creation was that if you lost your job through no fault of your own, the government would help you out for a few months while you look for a new job.

Third, the government created and filled 12 million jobs between 1934 and 1941. That's a major reform, because the idea of the government directly hiring people is something that had not been done before and has not been done, for example, in the current economic crisis.

And finally, new regulations on enterprises and laws governing taxes were passed. An example of the regulations was the Banking Act of 1933, which established that banks that accept deposits cannot be risk takers when it comes to investing that money. An example of a 1930s reform that affected tax laws was the increase in taxation of corporations and rich individuals. Taxes were raised on corporations and taxes were raised on rich people to help pay for these reforms.

What happened to these reforms? Where are they now when we need them to get through the current crisis? The answer to that question is, every single one of these reforms has been either weakened or eliminated.

The Banking Act was repealed by Congress and President Clinton in 1999. Eight years later, the overly risky investments by the largest U.S. banks led the country into the ongoing economic crisis. Similarly, the higher taxes on corporations and the rich that were levied in those years have all been reduced.

And consider the reform involved in the huge 1930s federal jobs program. In the current crisis there's not a word about federal employment. President Obama doesn't say a word about it, the Republicans don't mention it. It's as if it never happened. It's as if our entire political elite has had a mammoth case of amnesia in terms of what used to be basic policy. One of the greatest reforms of the 1930s—federal jobs to offset the inability or unwillingness of the private sector to hire—has vanished even though high unemployment needs it.

Then there's the great 1930s reform of creating the Social Security system. That reform is being whittled away now as benefits are reduced, eligibility tightened and costs raised.

The conclusion of this brief history is inescapable. The reforms of the 1930s, profoundly helpful to the mass of Americans, could not be sustained against the attacks of the wealthy few. The business interests whose profits were hurt by the reforms went to work to undo them. So too did the rich. The economic history of the last thirty-five years is the story of class war in the United States: how the 1 percent have erased or weakened key public benefits won by the 99 percent.

Reforms to deal with economic crises of the sort we're in now are at best temporary phenomenon. Yet all that's been done to this point in this crisis has been to re-introduce some of the reforms that we did in the 1930s. We haven't even dared to have federal employment but we have the Dodd–Frank Act to control financial markets, a little like the Banking Act. But if all we manage to do is pass a few limited reforms, here's what we know from our history. They will not survive. And even more likely, this time they will be gotten rid of even faster than they were last time because the wealthy will use their resources to have them repealed just as they have in the past.

What do I conclude? Reforms do not work or last in the way that we want them to, precisely because when we reform this economic system, we leave in place the institutions that will undo those reforms. What do I mean? There is no easy way to say this indirectly. I mean corporations. The people who run corporations, the handful of major shareholders together with a board of directors, they're the ones who gather into their hands the profits of our society. They're the ones who have the decision-making power over the productive apparatus of our economy. For them, every one of the reforms I've just mentioned has been a burden and an obstacle. Their job is to make money for themselves through the mechanism of the corporations they own or direct. They're hired to do that, they're paid to do that, they're rewarded in this system for doing that.

What does that mean? For them, a regulation that limits their profitability needs to be eliminated. A tax that takes from them what they would rather have as profits is to be reduced or eliminated. The burden of taking care of their workers' pension needs is to be reduced or eliminated. All of these things they work to evade, to weaken and, where possible, to eliminate. We can see time and again that corporations have used a portion of the profits they've made to weaken those laws, to eradicate those laws, to remove the burden of those taxes. And they've succeeded. And the last decades of U.S. history are a clear demonstration of the impact of the class war they have waged. The rich got richer while everyone else got poorer and the nation has been driven deeper and deeper into debt. And here we are.

Looking back, the shame is on the business community and the wealthy for attacking and erasing all progress made toward equality. The Republicans were the main party leading the plunder, but the Democrats proved unable or unwilling to challenge them. Looking forward, now that that we know what they're going to do, it would be shame on us for not having the will power, the clarity, and the courage to challenge the system. The Occupy movement is a surging statement that people across the nation see the need for new actions and organizations and movements that will begin to meet our needs, because nothing else is doing it.

Occupy corporations?

Absolutely. The answer is to change the corporation, to make a commitment that the democratic values we as Americans are supposed to endorse and uphold can and should begin in that place where most Americans spend most of their adult lives—at work. Five out of seven days, 9:00 to 5:00, millions are on the job. And if democracy is a value, then that's where it ought to exist. And it ought to be organized in our workplaces wherever they are: Our government offices, our factory floors, our stores, wherever it is.

The majority of the people, the workers, should be the ones who make the decisions. If we have to live with the decision of where the corporation is to be located, we have to be participants in making that decision. If we have to live with the decision of what kind of technology is used in the workplace, the air we breathe, the water we use, the toxicity of the chemicals, we have to live with the results, we have to participate. It can't be made by fifteen members of a board of directors meeting 1,000 miles away or a few major shareholders 10,000 miles away. That is not democracy, it's autocracy. Some call it plutocracy. Kingdoms used to work like that. If we're against that, which we say we are, then we ought to occupy the economy, challenge capitalism and democratize the enterprises.

Just to put a face on the economic crisis, there's an Associated Press story about a 92-year-old woman named Mary Power who is living "in a drafty trailer in Boston's West Roxbury neighborhood. She gets by on $11,000 a year in pension and Social Security benefits. Her heating-aid bill is skyrocketing. The assistance provided by the State of Massachusetts to her and to other indigent people is being reduced. She's saying, "'I will just have to crawl into bed with the covers over me and stay there. I will do what I have to do,' said Mary Power, a widow who has worked as a cashier and waitress until she was 80 years old." Just to put the kind of human touch beyond the economic numbers, which are very devastating.

A wise man once wrote years ago that you can tell a great deal about a society, gauge its fundamental cohesiveness and its ethics, by how it treats children and elderly. A society as wealthy as this one that condemns a 92-year-old woman to freezing during the winter is extraordinary. It tells you something more powerful about the social decline of the U.S. than any quantity of economic statistics that I could marshal to make that point. Imagine the face of the mayor of Boston or the governor of Massachusetts when confronted with a government he runs that can't do better than that for a woman who has spent a lifetime of work, who is 92 years of age, and who is discovering that because the government she has supported is unable or unwilling to tax the staggering wealth that is escaping taxation in this country today, she's going to have to spend her last days under the covers in a freezing, drafty trailer because this system doesn't work. It is a criticism of capitalism as a system that goes beyond blaming this or that politician or this or that industry. It's time to face the fact that our system doesn't work and to begin working on systemic solutions.

You've written an essay called "Evangelical Economics," which really talks about some of these faith-based beliefs in capitalism: Private property, the "invisible hand" that is somehow rectifying the market's volatility.

The "invisible hand" is the one I'd like to respond to, because in a way it's the foundational myth. It comes from Adam Smith, who in many ways is considered the father of modern economics as a discipline. He's famous, as is that phrase, written in the late eighteenth century. He was a professor of religion at the University of Edinburgh in Scotland. We don't have to have a powerful government, he argued against another famous British thinker, who was his nemesis, a man named Thomas Hobbes, the writer of *Leviathan*. Hobbes was arguing for a powerful government because if there weren't a powerful government, he said, we would all tear each apart in a horrific struggle of each against everyone else. This frightened and upset Adam Smith who feared powerful government. Smith said, No, we don't have to have a powerful leviathan government that controls us. And the reason we don't is that we have an economic system—and he meant capitalism—in which the following is true: If each person and each enterprise pursue their own self-interest, we will all be led—and here comes the phrase—as if by an invisible hand, to behavior, decisions, and actions that will lead to the greatest good of the greatest number.

This was a wonderfully comforting and compensating kind of argument. Smith was telling us all, we don't have to have a big, powerful government. We can afford to have an economic system without a powerful government because we have a system that works in such a way that we'll all be best off. Great. So suppose I try to get ahead by producing a commodity more cheaply than the next capitalist who then goes out of business and lays off his workers. I don't have to worry, I don't have to feel bad, I don't have to take any steps for that other one, because what I've done for my own self-interest will somehow work out for the best for everybody including that other destroyed business. You know what this is? This is a recipe for disregarding the consequences of your own actions. You're being told you don't have to worry about them because the system makes sure it all works out.

Even the most gullible among us ought at least to raise a skeptical eyebrow at Smith's argument.

But more than skepticism is in order here. Let me suggest you just look around. Are 25 million unemployed Americans a sign that if we all look out for our own self-interest, everything will all work out? Is one-third, almost, of our industry capacity sitting idle, gathering rust and dust, a sign that if everybody pursues their own self-interest, it will all work out? When you look around and see the gaps between those who are struggling and those living in luxury, are you convinced that this is a system where everything is working out? Come on. Adam Smith's idea was silly. It was a thin veneer on justifying the existing distribution of wealth and income, on justifying the status quo, and the capitalist organization of enterprises, and everybody out there striving to make a buck, by telling us it would all work out for the best.

We do not have a system that is the best of all possible worlds that is led by an invisible hand, by God, to the best outcome. Every society before us has struggled and become a better place because people had the courage to criticize what was wrong. We badly need that in the U.S. today.

You've written that Mexico " is an increasingly dysfunctional economy. Signs of social explosions are proliferating." What are the characteristics of Mexican capitalism that brought you to these conclusions?

Mexico has always had a complicated, difficult, and in

many ways tragic relationship with the United States. The U.S. is its large northern neighbor, much richer, much more developed, much larger, much more militarily powerful, all of that. So Mexico has always existed, a little bit like Canada, in the shadow of its larger neighbor.

Over the last thirty years, that relationship, always difficult, became even more difficult and peculiar. But it had a positive impact on Mexico for a while, if you understand the word "positive" in the following way. From the 1970s to 2007, the U.S. experienced, for a variety of reasons, a boom in its housing market. It also experienced the formation of a common market among Canada, the U.S. and Mexico. As a result, Mexico underwent a dramatic economic change.

First, it got invaded by American corporations that are bigger and richer than their Mexican counterparts. Instead of literally tens of thousands of small stores scattered across the villages of Mexico, in comes Wal-Mart, establishing megastores every few miles, wiping out countless Mexicans' livelihoods because they could not compete with what those megastores offer. Second, the influx of U.S. products undercut local Mexican production, as in the case of corn, for example, a staple of the Mexican diet. And finally, an opportunity for some Mexican producers to sell into the U.S. market created jobs in those few areas where the Mexican companies could produce exports for the United States. In short, it shook up Mexico's economy, depriving millions of Mexicans of the opportunity to continue making a livelihood anymore inside Mexico, but benefiting a few Mexican capitalists consolidating into that market. Suddenly the rich in Mexico became much richer but the mass of Mexicans became more hopelessly entrenched in poverty.

As this played itself out, these poorer Mexicans faced a dire choice. Literally, if they were to survive, they would either have to become burdens on their family, friends, and villages, or they would have to leave Mexico. Public services in Mexico are unreliable or simply do not exist in many parts of Mexico, particularly in the many indigenous areas of the country. Thus, many working-age people did what you might expect them to do—they left in search of work. They migrated to the United States. That worked for a while, because the U.S. had a housing boom, because the U.S. was full of employers who were eager to hire undocumented Mexican immigrants because you could pay them less, you could keep them off the books, you wouldn't have to make Social Security and other kinds of contributions for them. They were a cheap, exploitable source of labor. And at a time when unemployment was not terrible, the U.S. working class could be persuaded to look the other way or at least to make minimum resistance. So millions of Mexicans flooded north. This eased a big problem for Mexico—what to do with people, millions of them, for whom Mexico could provide and Mexican capitalism could provide no jobs.

The exodus of working people benefited Mexico from the 1980s right up until around 2007. Those Mexicans who left and got a job in the U.S. lived very frugally, lived very simply. Even though they didn't earn much, they did what generations of immigrants have always done: They saved money and they sent it back home. During the 1990s and early part of this century, what we call remittances, the money Mexican immigrants in the U.S. sent back to Mexico, was the second or third most important income-generating export of that country, crucial to the Mexican economy.

So Mexico solved two problems: it solved the problem of unemployed people, which would have been a tremendous drag on the economy; and it saw a massive inflow of money as those exported Mexican workers sent money back home to their families, relatives, boyfriends, girlfriends and so forth. That was the good news.

But when the economic crisis hit the United States, Mexico's exports of people no longer made any sense. Since the housing market collapsed in the middle of 2007, it has not been allowed or helped to recover. Very few houses are built relative to the number that used to be built. Very few houses are building extensions. No part of the housing market is booming. Therefore, those Mexicans who had been hired can no longer find work. And in a time of unemployment and a time of growing hostility to immigrants, particularly undocumented ones, many Mexican people are basically heading home to Mexico. They don't qualify for U.S. unemployment benefits because they worked under the table. They don't qualify for all kinds of other benefits because they're not citizens. And they're afraid of dealing with the government for fear that their undocumented status will lead them into jail or into deportation or both. So they go back to Mexico, to a country that has no jobs for them, as it hasn't for years. They're going back to conditions that are as bad as they are here except that in most places it's not as cold in the winter and there may be a family or a friend to help them in ways that they don't have in the United States.

Compounding Mexico's problems is the fact that the return of working people has dried up the river of remittances—the steady source of money sent from Mexicans in the U.S. to their families in Mexico. All that money that used to come into Mexico to offset the money that the rich have taken is simply drying up. This is a one-two punch that has decimated the Mexican economy: Millions of people returning who have no work, millions of dollars that used to flow into the economy not coming in anymore. Either one of those would have been a body blow to the Mexican economy. The combination of both of them over the same few years has rendered Mexico a failed government, a failed state. That's why we're reading all the time about massive pitched battles between "drug cartels" and "police forces," when the story, if read to the end, indicates that the boundary line between these two is—how shall I say?—fuzzy and permeable in a remarkable way.

Nothing is happening to improve this situation. We have a slow-motion bomb exploding on our southern border that can transform our lives, the politics of these two countries, the politics of the entire Western hemisphere. This is a catastrophe. It has only been kept from the American people by the political peculiarity that as these people become unemployed, instead of facing that problem here, we export the people and the problem back to Mexico, which means the problem explodes there first and then the shock waves hit us here in one form or another.

One sees in occasional media reports that China and India will somehow revive the economies in the U.S. and Europe. You actually warn about these notions as fantasies, and you call this kind of thinking a diversion. Why do you say that?

Here's the problem. Over the last twenty years in the case of China and at least the last ten in the case of India, the economic growth in those societies has been much more robust, much faster than that in the United States or Western Europe. So, of course, attention has focused on these societies as examples of capitalist economies, which they are, really. In both countries, even though in China it's called a communist country or a socialist country, they are basically becoming more and more private-enterprise capitalist economies, even more than they were before. Attention has focused on them because they are the few capitalist "success stories" that recent history has made possible.

This has led some enthusiasts to take an immense further step, which I don't think is justified, and that is to imagine that not only are they having success when everybody else in the capitalist world is not, but that they are somehow capable of independently continuing that success even as the rest of the world suffers a prolonged depression. That's where I think fantasy comes in.

First, India and China are sizable economies but smaller and weaker than the U.S. and Western Europe (separately or together), especially if you look at it in terms of per capita, relative to their populations, which is how you should look at it. Second, success for both India and China is heavily dependent on their exports, and particularly on their exports to the U.S. and Europe. So that if the U.S. and Europe have a prolonged economic downturn, that undermines economic well-being in India and China, because they can't proceed to do well if their exports to Europe and the U.S. falter. To say this another way, to use economic language, there is no independent development anymore in a globalized economy, where we all depend, in complicated, multiple ways, on one another. Economic decline in the two richest economic units of the world, Western Europe and the U.S., will negatively impact everywhere else although unevenly in time and across locations.

Part of the gain of China, which is much more important than the gain of India, is a very typical phenomenon of economic downturn periods. In economic downturns, for example, here in the U.S., we see people who no longer can afford to shop at middle-income kinds of stores such as Macy's and Sears—and those stores have a had very hard times. For example, early in 2012 Sears announced closing hundreds of stores because they simply couldn't make it. However, if you look at the cheaper discount stores—Target, Wal-Mart, dollar stores—they can do well for a while. Not independent of the economy, but exactly because the economy is in such terrible shape, they gain because they pick up the customers who can't afford anything else. China is partly like that. China can keep exporting for a while because it is a low-cost goods producer. India can do likewise because it is a low-cost producer of services.

However, there are limits to this. After a while, especially in long-lasting downturns like the present, the people who used to be able to buy the cheaper products will not be able to continue. Indeed, in 2012 many observers of China believe that economy will have a serious downturn, and much of the debate only hangs on whether it will be a "hard landing" or a "soft landing," which are economic terms for saying the decline in China will be extreme and short or will be gradual in its impact.

So I think it a fantasy to imagine these economies leading the world into new prosperity. It's a diversion, it's a way to avoid facing the reasons inside the U.S. and inside Europe that are causing the world economy to be in such trouble and looking for salvation somewhere else.

Speaking of empire, are U.S. plans to maintain hundreds of military bases on foreign soil around the world compatible with its pronounced economic weakness?

I'm afraid that in the minds of most U.S. leaders it's seen a little bit differently. That the growing political and economic weaknesses or, let's put it differently, declines in the previous period's economic and political strengths, are causing more, not less, emphasis on the military. The U.S. military's global footprint is now increasingly out of whack, out of balance, with the nation's larger economic and political situation. In the history of the world, that's a dangerous arrangement. Countries in that situation have historically been tempted to try to recoup their former political and economic glories by using the military cards they can still play. In a sense, the United States is already doing that. By maintaining a global system of bases far larger than any other country—no other country is even close—by spending more money on its military than any other nations on Earth, by having an arsenal of nuclear weapons far out of line with that of any other country, and by showing itself able and willing to send hundreds of thousands of troops halfway around the world to Iraq, Afghanistan, and so on, the U.S. is playing the card that nobody else in the world can play.

But it's a very peculiar card, because it's one thing to wages wars in Iraq and Afghanistan because they are weak forces in world politics. So you can't really use your weapon where it most is needed. That's not lost on the people who see it as perhaps—dare one say it—a kind of paper tiger one is facing here. That requires the U.S. to try to make it more credible, that it will use this weapon. This is a very danger-ous, tit-for-tat, cat-and-mouse game and it's not clear that the U.S. can afford to play it. Meanwhile, the imbalance grows as the relative political and military strength of non-U.S. players in the world economy grows. And that is not just Europe and China. It's also India, it's also places like Brazil, Russia and so on, that are carving out strategies, tra-jectories, and places in the world economy that are growing at the expense of the United States in many ways.

Internal to the U.S. you have this phenomenon of a competition among the states by giving incentives at workers' expenses and taxpayers' expenses to lure corporations, all in the pursuit of jobs. They call this "a race to the bottom," where corporations are attracted to states with low wages, no unions, no environmental regulations, etc.

That's been a reality here in the U.S. for a long time. Years ago I attended meetings in several U.S. cities. in which I watched with horror as a naïve young man, the "economic development officer" of city A, tried to convince a corporation to locate its new factory in his town. That was followed by the "economic development officer" from city B saying, "No, no, no. Don't go to city A's location. We've got a better deal. We will give you no taxes to pay for twelve years. He only will give you no taxes to pay for six years. We will provide you with a new road built to your factory so that your trucks can get in and out. They won't do that." Of course, as each city and town competes with every other, they try and outdo each other. And in the end it's the community who pays for it. So it means the city government will have to tax everybody else more or the city government will have to cut out social services it provided to people so it can instead provide costly incentives to attract corporations.

What's been new during the last twenty-five years has been the globalization of that process. Corporations not only pit U.S. cities against each other, but also against those from developing nations like Nigeria and Malaysia. These countries face such desperate problems, that they offer to outdo the U.S. cities, and lower environmental restrictions are often part of the package. Here is that race to the bottom, as others have called it, because what the end result will be is that every community, city, every state, every government around the world will have to raise taxes on its people or cut back social services to those people to free up the money to give away to the corporations.

An audit of the Fed revealed a rather sharp discrepancy on the size of the bank bailout. What do you know about that?

In the final months of 2011 a court case that had been begun, as far as I understand, by the Bloomberg financial news service was decided in favor of Bloomberg and against and over the opposition for two years of the Federal Reserve. Bloomberg wanted information, as many senators and congressmen and congresswomen had asked for, informing everyone of what is called in financial language transparency. That is, we're supposed to know what the central bank of every country is doing, because it's necessary for the decisions businesses, banks, politicians, and citizens make. The public supposedly has a right to know. So Bloomberg demanded to know, on behalf of everybody else, how much money had the Fed given and to which banks and others in the depths of the economic crisis that started in the middle of 2008 and basically has gone on ever since. The Fed refused. It withheld the information. That made Bloomberg go to the courts to force, under the Freedom of Information Act and other statutes, the release of that information.

When it finally came out, the information was a bombshell, and it was duly reported not only by the Bloomberg service that had won the information but also by a whole host of other examiners and commentators. Who got the money? How much money was involved? The estimates varied. The

Federal Reserve came up with a figure in the neighborhood of $1.7 trillion. Bloomberg, in its stories, came up with a radically different figure—$7.7 trillion. That's quite a difference. We're not in the same ballpark here. And other commentators, both governmental and private, have since then come up with a whole variety of estimates, some as high as $25 trillion.

It depends a little bit on how you count. One way to count is simply to say, what was the largest amount of money outstanding from the Fed at any one moment. That will get you a small number. A different way of counting is counting the total, adding up the total outstanding each day, because sometimes the Federal Reserve provides money for a day, sometimes for a week, sometimes for a month, and so on. If you add it all up, of course, you're going to get a much larger number because it's the total amount outstanding.

In the end, why quibble over this? The important point is that the major private banks of the world—and these are the ones that the Fed did most of its business with—were defunct, could not function, could not and did not trust one another. They had ceased to be able to do their business. And they couldn't help each other and they couldn't help themselves to survive. So they all went in a great rush to the United States Treasury and to the Federal Reserve, the most powerful financial agencies in the world, to bail them out, to hand over huge amounts of money, over and over and over again. Borrowing billions on Monday, paying it back on Thursday, needing to go back to the Federal Reserve the following Monday to get it for a couple of weeks, a couple of hours, whatever it was. But they did this over and over *for years*. We didn't have a capitalist banking system. We had a socialized, nationalized banking system. A banking system that could not work had it not benefited to the tune of trillions and trillions of dollars of our tax money from the Treasury and trillions more from the Federal Reserve.

Some people are shocked when they discover that the Federal Reserve Bank had provided this kind of financial help not just to U.S. banks but to Swiss, French, German, and other countries' leading institutions. That's an important thing to understand because it's a lesson in the structure of today's global economy. The big banks of the world do much of their business with one another. They borrow from one another, they lend to one another and they guarantee and insure one another's loans in a variety of the ways. Therefore, if the banking system ceases to function, it doesn't matter anymore which bank starts the process. It's an instantaneous chain reaction. If the Morgan Stanley Bank in New York is suddenly unable to continue its business, that throws the UBS Bank in Switzerland or the BNP Paribas bank in Paris into an immediate crisis because they have loans out to Morgan Stanley which they can't get repaid. So if you're going to salvage the capitalist banking system, you have to pump money in, which is what the Federal Reserve did, to everybody who is at risk of being unable to function and thereby jeopardize the global credit system.

It's a little bit like airport problems in the United States. If a terrible snowstorm hits the Chicago airport, you won't be able to fly from Phoenix to Dallas. That's not because there's any snow there. It's because the airplanes that go to Phoenix have to go through Chicago. As a result, they can't find the landing place or they can't get the fuel they need and therefore they can't go to St. Louis, so they can't make the exchange with another airplane that will go and pick you up in Phoenix. You have to discover that you're dependent on things happening far away, with other airlines, in other airports.

It's the same thing with the international financial system. What we need to understand most of all is this: When a banking system produces the kind of crisis through its speculations, its asset-backed securities, its credit default swaps, its extensive loans, its inadequate reserves—and all of these have been documented—when a capitalist banking system badly malfunctions in this way so that the pursuit of self-interest by each bank doesn't produce, through the "invisible hand," the best outcome but produces global destabilization and crisis, you have removed the justification for there being a private banking system. If the only way to save and sustain the capitalist banking system is through handouts from a government welfare program, then something serious has to change.

We shouldn't have private banks. We should have a public banking system that helps communities, enterprises, and people, a publicly accountable system that is open and transparent, so that we do not have the risk of them waltzing us into such a crisis yet again. And if credit crises were still to occur, it would be public money bailing out public banks in a publicly transparent way. It is a shame and scandal to have bailed out these capitalist institutions with public money and then to turn back over to them the same private banking system that failed us, that cost us, and that now laughs at its ability to have done all that damage and to escape with nothing more than a handful of half-baked Dodd–Frank regulations.

In the case of all of this money that was given to these various banks by the Fed, has the Fed been paid back? Do we know that yet?

Some of the programs administered by the Fed were loans that have been paid back. Others are loans that have not been paid back. Others are guarantees of other people's debts, where you can't count in terms of payback. The Federal Reserve has created vast new quantities of money. It has done this by literally printing more money, but mostly by simply giving credits to banks, saying to a bank, "You had $10 billion in your account with us. Now you have $50 billion." So the bank can now do things with this money that the Federal Reserve just electronically created. This means that the quantity of money floating around the system in the hands of private banks and others and available for them to spend has been enormously increased. That money, if it ever gets spent, will drive up prices. We will have that inflation that worried folks see lurking in the background.

When you put all this together, it is simply misleading to talk about the Federal Reserve as in some sense having "gotten paid." We don't yet know the cost of all that money creation. We can't easily measure the cost of providing all those short-term loans to desperate banks that were deemed too big to fail. It's equally difficult to count the costs incurred to all Americans by the historically unprecedented period of extremely low interest rates created by the Fed to support the capitalist banks and their profitability for the last several years. The notion of having been "paid back" is simply a misleading claim aimed to de-escalate the public's correct sense of outrage at welfare for the capitalists that was not made similarly available to the families and people who are unable to pay their heating bills, rent or mortgages.

If we also factor in the ways that the U.S. Treasury has also provided all kinds of supports, it's safe to say that trillions in public funds have been used to assist the capitalist system that has waged class war on the public for three decades, lowering wages, firing workers and altering the Tax Code to further enrich the few, with less benefits for the many. It couldn't be more clear: this system does not work. It took pride in itself in the decades before 2007, saying all kind of nonsense about how the government is a burden, the government shouldn't intrude, the private sector knows best, guarantees growth. All lies. All false. We ought to face the fact that we now know that was all false, that it was the same people giving those speeches who rushed to get the government to save them and bail them out. The lesson from that is we shouldn't have a private sector that works that way. And it is a shame on us that we do not yet produce the political movement strong enough to generate debate over all these facts on a national level.

Does the word "socialism" as used in U.S. political and media discourse have any relation to its meaning?

No. In the U.S. the word "socialism," the word "communism," "Marxism," "collectivism" and a whole bunch of others are treated like derogatory words, words that are so negative that nobody ever has to define them. You just shake your head to show that you're in agreement that these are bad words. It's a little bit like religious people referring to words like "hell" or "the devil" or things like that.

So I think we're going to need in the U.S.A. a whole new generation of people not brought up during the Cold War or in the legacy of the Cold War, able to think for themselves and able to discover a single simple fact. Throughout the history of capitalism, from its beginnings to today, there have been people able and willing to see the flaws, to see the failures, and to make criticisms of capitalism. If that comes as a shock, it's because you've lived in a society that's been afraid of discussing socialism and communism in reasonable, balanced ways for half a century. That half of a century is now over. The disappearance of the Soviet Union and the crisis in global capitalism since 2007 provide the world with two major reasons to stop thinking of socialism in simplistic terms. As people recognize the limits and failures of capitalism, they're going to begin to reexamine what the alternatives are, and the alternatives most studied and attempted over the last 150 years have been one or another variety of socialism and communism.

You make a distinction between socialism and communism.

It's a distinction that comes out of the history of these alternatives. The first alternative that was talked about in most of the world from roughly the middle of the nineteenth century to the 1917 revolution in Russia was socialism. That was the word used by Marx and Engels and by the major theorists in this area. "Socialist" was the name taken by the political parties that wanted to go beyond capitalism in many countries around the world between 1850 and 1920.

As a result of the 1917 revolution, the Soviet Union became the first country to try to organize and institutionalize a non-capitalist system in a big country. Doing so produced, as all such historically new efforts do, a legion of critics and a legion of supporters. They argued. Were developments in Soviet Russia really the realization of socialism or were they a distortion of socialism? Intense debates led to a split among socialists. The split over many issues basically focused on one overwhelming issue: Did you support the USSR in its particular institutionalization of socialism, or did you not? If you supported the Soviet Union, you took a new name, communist, like the name taken by the USSR's leading political party. If you did not, you held on to the old name, socialist. So, for example, here in the U.S. and in many other countries, the large socialist party basically split into what remained a socialist party, generally critical of the Soviet Union, and what became the Communist Party, generally supportive. So the difference is a matter of degree, a matter of political history at a particular time, less than a matter of the fundamental ideas.

The notion in both cases of socialists and communists, although they disagree about the degree, is that private enterprise harms the public. Enterprises should be owned and operated in the name of and by the people, usually understood as the government taking over in the name of the people, running enterprises. The second idea was that instead of an unregulated market, you have planning. The government, representing the people, should plan the distribution of resources and products. Instead of a capitalist market in which goods are distributed according to how much money you have to spend, goods are distributed according to need.

Thus, what became the two key dividing lines between socialism and communism, on the one hand, and capitalism, on the other, was 1) state property versus private property, and 2) planning versus markets. I think all of those distinctions are going to have to be revisited by the critics of capitalism, rediscovered by them, evaluated, and further developed.

This is already happening in many parts of the United States. For example, the Occupy movement has initiated a number of discussion groups, meetings, talk shows, teach-ins, Web sites and publications. People now want more than just a critique of capitalism's subversion of democracy and the public interest, people want actionable alternatives. And since there are such deep feelings of negativity, by and large, for the actual alternatives that existed in Russia, Eastern Europe, China, and elsewhere, often for very good reasons, they are interested in knowing about them but also in being balanced, assessing their failures, and coming up with what now ought to be the learned alternative to capitalism. I think that's where people will go. It's a naïve and head-in-the-sand kind of mentality to pretend we don't have to learn from or know about earlier efforts to go beyond capitalism. However critical we are, we have to learn from them, both what they achieved and where they failed, so that we can do better today.

You've said of the Soviet revolution that it had in effect replaced private capitalists with state-appointed ones.

Whatever the merits of planning over markets—and I personally am persuaded of this—a reasonable system has to use both of these mechanisms. It cannot be a one-sided focus on planning without the use of markets, and it's equally absurd to go to the other extreme. In fact, most societies mix planning and non-planning, planning and markets, in various combinations. And I would hope that a reasonable and rational society would do that, with a place for market trading, for letting people freely come to agreements with one another about what they buy and sell—I think there is some point to that—but also to plan things in the interests of the community, and there's certainly a lot of point to that as well.

Perhaps the most important lesson is that the past experiments with socialism and communism, with their focus on planning rather than markets and on socialized property rather than private property, overlooked the radical transformation of the enterprise itself. Here's where my point about the Soviet Union enters. They got rid of the private boards of directors, they got rid of the private shareholders, they closed the stock market. But they did not turn over these enterprises to be run by the workers in them through institutions and mechanisms of democracy. What they did instead was dismiss the old, private boards of directors and they replaced them with state officials. So instead of fifteen people running the company who were selected by the shareholders, you had fifteen people who were selected by the government or by the Communist Party.

That was definitely a change with important social consequences. But it also left the mass of people inside each enterprise in a little-changed subordinate position, having to live with the top-down decisions made by state officials but being excluded from participating in those decisions in any organic, real way. That, to me, is a crucial part of getting beyond capitalism. If you leave the structure in place and only change the people at the top from privately elected boards of directors to publicly selected state officials, you've gotten rid of private capitalism, but you still have the same structure in the enterprise. I call that state capitalism, because it's state officials that have replaced the private boards of directors. I'm not saying that's a bad change to make, I'm not even saying that might not be an advance in certain ways. But it isn't what I understand socialism and communism to be. It isn't a break in the way I think a break has to be made.

Let me illustrate this in a way I find helpful. The founders of this country didn't decide to get rid of kings and queens by putting in somebody else who is a king and a queen. The founders said, "No more kings and queens." They wanted a new set of social relations free of that hierarchy. To this day, we in the U.S. pride ourselves on having, or at least in theory having, a system of checks and balances: a Supreme Court that is checked by a Congress that is checked by a president. They keep each other in check. We don't want power concentrated in a tiny number of people, let alone one, so we make it a larger number of people that are accountable to one another and to the public in some way. I think that's a step in the right direction. I don't think it goes anywhere near far enough, but it's a step.

If that step is appropriate for our politics, it's also appropriate for many other aspects of our national well-being, including our economic system. We should not have a handful of people at the top deciding what a corporation does, no chief executive who has in his hands the decision-making power that tens and hundreds of thousands of workers have to live with. That's autocracy. Some call it plutocracy-rule of the rich. It's really a form of economic monarchy. It's incompatible with the public interest and genuine democracy, and is therefore something we ought to get rid of, just as much as we ought to have gotten rid of and did get rid of kings and queens and other kinds of autocrats.

I'd go further. Many Americans are dissatisfied to indignant about our political system. People are angry about having their interests ignored, with how easily political leaders get distracted from what they ought to be doing, with the degree to which they are self-serving and corrupt. This is what drove the Occupy movement from Zuccotti Park to over a thousand sites around the world, and why over 6,000 people have been arrested at Occupy protests during its first few months organizing. People are at the boiling point.

A concern being articulated more and more loudly is that we don't have the economic democracy that could keep our political democracy honest. People, for example, have not participated in local politics because they haven't acquired the skills or experience to do so. If workers learned 9:00 to 5:00, Monday through Friday, to be skilled in workplace diplomacy and in collectively designing enterprise functions and growth, in reaching and implementing collective decisions, in correcting mistakes as a collective decision-making body, they would not only know how to do that in their communities where they live, they would insist on it. They would participate, they would keep informed, because they learned how important participation and being informed is to running the businesses for which they're responsible and upon which they financially depend. Among the great early achievements of the Occupy movement is not just putting the gross inequalities of our economic system on the national agenda, but experimenting with forms of direct democracy that can transform neighborhoods, communities, and the country as a whole.

So I think that one of the ways we will move our political democracy from mere rituals and formalities of corporate-financed elections to the reality of real decision making by the people involved is to democratize the economic sphere. We should have done that all along. Occupy the economy. It's a minimum commitment to democracy, and it will help expedite the spread of genuine democracy to the rest of our society as well.

Could you talk about workers' councils in relation to economic democracy?

The term "workers' council" comes directly from the Italy where important efforts were made to realize such councils under the leadership of Antonio Gramsci. Examples can be found in many countries, including here in the United States, where genuine democracy takes over the operation of enterprises and of governments, too. We call them co-ops most of the time, like the Park Slope Food Co-op in Brooklyn, for example. Stores, factories, craft shops where workers say, We don't want a boss, we don't want a corporation, we don't want a dividing line, a wall, between those who do the work and those who make the decisions about what, where and how to produce and what to do with the profits. We want, instead, a cooperative enterprise, a collective enterprise, a community enterprise. And they've done that. Coops have included people who are religious, because often religions support cooperative enterprises. Coops have also included people who are stalwarts of the Republican Party who think of all of coops as an ingenious entrepreneurial innovation. Co-ops can also be as diverse as the U.S. itself. For example, on any given day at the Park Slope Food Co-op in Brooklyn you may find a Jamaican man in dreadlocks laboring side by side with a co-worker who is a member of Brooklyn's orthodox Hasidic community.

Throughout the history of the United States and every other capitalist country the desire of workers to be their own bosses rather than work under other bosses is deep and abiding and keeps resurfacing. In a way, the idea of realizing genuine democracy in our economy of the same sort we see at Occupy movement's general assemblies is the idea of making a serious effort for the first time in human history to generalize a new way of doing business in which the workers who do the work also make the decisions on the job.

Socialism in the U.S. actually has a rich history. One of its publications, for example, was Appeal to Reason, *which had 700,000 subscribers at one point, over 4 million readers. The great, legendary socialist, Eugene Victor Debs, once ran for president from his jail cell. He got a million votes. Wilson put Debs in jail because he was opposed to U.S. entry into World War I. So there is that rich historical background here, of which many people are unaware. I also remember Howard Zinn once telling me that one of the great blows to socialism was when the USSR appropriated that word, thereby tarnishing it in many people's minds.*

All words that are important in history have been picked up and used by all kind of characters, for all kinds of reasons. It's not unusual that that happened to socialism. In fact, it would have been unique if it had not happened to socialism. And the same is true for capitalism.

Let me give you an example to drive the point home. The dictator of Chile for many, many years, a man named

Pinochet, loved to refer to his society as "a society of freedom." Heads of the apartheid regime in South Africa often referred to South Africa as one of the "freedom-loving" states of the world. Every dictator I know of boasts of the freedom his regime has brought to his people. The word "freedom" has been abused, taken over by all sorts of people whose meaning in using that term we should find abhorrent. Yet that doesn't mean that we should give up on the concept of freedom or decide never to use it again. We insist on retaining a concept of freedom, making it central in our society, and having at least some discussions and debates about what it means, how it is used and abused and what it ought to mean.

People who say that the Soviet Union abused socialism, that's fine. That's a point of view I understand. But it is not an argument to stop talking about socialism, any more than it would have been an argument to say we mustn't discuss freedom anymore because Pinochet referred to his own dictatorial regime in that language.

What about the relevance of the ideas of Marx, who died more than 125 years ago, in terms of alienation in relation to work and class and class struggle?

Marx, like the word socialism, has been abused and Marx's writings have been peculiarly interpreted.

Let me make it clear. Marx never wrote about communism and socialism. It wasn't a topic he felt he had the expertise or the interest to write about. He felt that was for the future. What Marx was interested in and devoted all of his mature writing to was analyzing capitalism, the system in which he lived and we live now. How did he analyze it? He analyzed it as a critic. He analyzed it as someone who thought way back in the 1800s that the world could do better than capitalism.

Marx is the preeminent critic of capitalism. A lot of people have picked up on his writing, so there's a whole tradition and literature of criticism rooted in his analysis. Why in the world would a serious student of capitalism not consider Marx's arguments? Perhaps because of fear, one-sided thinking, or a really poor education. More likely because of the decades upon decades of bias against it. An economic system and an educational system that systematically exclude the voices of their critics do not deserve respect. To this day, the writings of Marx demonstrate an exquisite critical understanding of capitalism. Students should know they have to go out and work on their own to rectify the deficiency of an educational system that works that way.

Even minimal psychological awareness would suggest that we ought to question an economic system that is factually proven to enrich the already wealthy while destabilizing the rest of society as our wealthy have been enriched and our society has been destabilized. Marx and Marxism remain a rich repository of critical analyses of and programs to do better than capitalism. Any balanced assessment of modern capitalism must include consideration of that set of ideas, proposals, and discussions of the world's efforts to date to go beyond capitalism.

Is class struggle a relevant term?

Absolutely. It depends, however, on what you mean by "class." And there is no term in the English language that I am aware of about which there is so little consensus, so little shared understanding. The word "class" as a noun comes from a verb. The verb is "to classify." And all it means is to take a population—it could be a population of candies, a population of dog bones, a population of buttons—and to break them into groups, to classify them—red buttons versus blue buttons, large buttons versus small buttons, large people versus small people, brown-skinned people versus yellow-skinned people, whatever. So all that class means is a subdivision, a class of any group. There are different classes because you can break them into several groups. For example, the people over 6 feet are the class of tall people, the people between 5 and 6 feet are the class of medium-height people, and then there is the class of short people, etc.

So let's turn to economics, where things are classified, too. Way back in ancient Greece, a long time ago, people broke down populations into subgroups called classes. The ancient Greeks were particularly interested in two kinds of classifications, breaking down their societies into two kinds of groups. The first classification focused on property ownership: The class of people who owned versus the class of people who didn't. The rich and the poor; the propertied versus those who own no property. They made sense of their society by talking about the relationships between these two subgroups, these two classes. When, for example, those who had little wanted to have more and those who had more didn't want to give any of it up, then there could be a struggle occurring between the two classes of people over the distribution of property.

The second ancient use of the term class was not about property but about power. The question was not what you owned but the question was, what authority do you have? Are you an order giver or are you an order taker? Are you in the class of rulers or in the class that's ruled? Who tells whom what to do about what? Thus class struggle refers to the people who speak out, organize and act to challenge the ways power and authority are wielded to their disadvantage. The struggle for democracy, for example, is often a struggle about power, about the conditions and relations of ruling and ruled classes. In short, then, there have been class struggles over property and class struggles over power.

Marx, writing in the nineteenth century, made use of those ideas, as have many other people including Thomas Jefferson, Thomas Paine and dozens of others around the world. But Marx's use involved also identifying a new and different concept of class that was not based in ownership or power. He reasoned that in all human communities, when members produce the goods and services without which the community can't live, it is always only some of the members that do the productive work. Those productive workers always generate a surplus, an output larger than what they themselves consume.

And here comes Marx's punch line. In every human community the question has to be asked and the decision has to be made, who gets that surplus? One option is that the workers who produce it themselves get it and decide what to do with it. But, Marx says, in capitalism that's not the way it works. In capitalism the people who produce the surplus don't get it. Somebody else gets it, and that somebody else is a capitalist. The capitalist decides what to do with that surplus—whether to plow it back into the business, whether to pay themselves fortunes of salaries, whether to hire lawyers, whether to do a big advertising campaign. You produce it and they decide what to do with it. That fundamental injustice and inequality is not only deplored by Marx on moral, ethical, and political grounds, which he does, but he also proceeds to show that one of the reasons we have periodic crises is that the way those capitalists use that surplus builds crisis into the system.

In the Marxian view of capitalism and the current economic structure that we're functioning in, is the relationship between the owner and the worker inherently adversarial? Is there any way to change that, or is that something intrinsic to that dynamic?

Let's be careful here. The basic adversarial relationship today is between the worker who produces the surplus and the board of directors of modern capitalist corporations. Those boards are today's receivers of the surpluses produced by most workers. Those boards distribute the surpluses as they and the major shareholders who select them see fit. Boards of directors are not necessarily—and usually not—also the owners of the corporations. Those are rather the shareholders. You need to be very careful here. Ownership in modern capitalism is separate from who the capitalist is. The owner has become relatively passive. What owners do is own shares of stock. Typically what they're interested in is getting a dividend from the stock they own and maybe being able to sell the stock at a higher price than they paid for it. What the company actually does is not their concern or responsibility. They're tangentially interested, because they don't want the company to go out of business or make mistakes, but basically they're at a remove.

For the producers of the surplus, their adversary is the board of directors. And here the adversarial relationship is crystal clear. First of all, the more your employer pays you per hour, the less is left for him. If you produce $25 worth of stuff for every hour you work, if the employer pays you $20, the employer nets $5. If the employer can pay you only $15, the employer gets to keep $10. The more the employer can drive down workers' pay, the more profit, the more surplus, the employer gets into his hands and the more secure and the more successful the capitalist corporation becomes. So right at the get-go there is a contradiction, a conflict.

That's why all capitalists throughout history are interested in finding ways to reduce the wage bill they have to pay, either by replacing workers with machines or by moving production to places where workers' wages are lower, or by replacing male with female workers, adult workers with child workers, citizen workers with undocumented immigrant workers, and so on. That's why capitalists are always seeking and finding new ways to take away benefits, shift this or that business cost on to workers, make workers work harder, faster, and so on. Each board of directors' creditors, shareholders and competitors pressure it to squeeze more surplus out of the workers. Some capitalists come to enjoy a kind of combat mentality: I'm going to defeat the workers' opposition to producing more surplus. Other capitalists don't want to hurt the workers at all; they try to explain that they are being competed against by other capitalists and have no real choice. This crazy logic of capitalism is true. The competition among capitalists often does drive down wages. Conflicts between capitalists and workers are thus endemic, built into the system. The interests of the classes are opposed, and class struggles ignite.

Then Marx, a very sophisticated thinker, takes this analysis one big step further. He points out that what capitalists do to survive—drive down wages—actually also undercuts capitalists ability to survive. Why? Because capitalists have to sell their workers' output to survive. And most of the people who buy workers' output in capitalist societies are the workers. If capitalists succeed in lowering the wages, they diminish workers' capacity to buy what capitalists have to sell.

Capitalists have been torn by this contradiction from day one. Marx uses the contradiction and capitalism's various and often wasteful and/or unsuccessful ways of dealing with it as argument for why modern societies can and should do better than capitalism as their economic system. Capitalists and most of their defenders tend to pretend that there is no contradiction. They deny that their system doesn't have these problems, so we are forced to live with the contradictions and problems while they deny them. It's a little bit like parents who deny that there's any tension between them, but their children have to live in that tension, and it's only worse because the parents deny it.

We are living through capitalism's crisis since 2007 because capitalists, having been quite successful in holding down wages and changing tax codes in their own favor, discovered that the mass of people can't afford to borrow much more and can not therefore afford to buy the way they used to, can't afford to service their own debt, and that's bringing the system down. But the grave injustice for the 99 percent is that despite the crisis, the 1 percent are so much better off than everybody else that they can still weather the crisis in plush luxury. While tens of millions lose their income, the capitalists can ride out the crisis and still come out with great wealth and power.

Explain a bit about Friedrich Engels and his relationship with Marx. And following Engels' model, explore what has to change inside socialism to improve it.

Marx and Engels were collaborators. They became friends as adults; they hadn't known each other before. They saw eye to eye on many things and they wrote many pieces together. There's a whole industry of analytics that tries to show that they had differences, which they did, and that they were in some cases opponents on some questions. But they were lifelong friends. If you ever doubt that, just read the eulogy Engels articulated when Marx died. Marx died in

1883; Engels lived until 1895. It's a moving tribute of one great thinker to another.

The thing that is for me most interesting about Engels was that he was a bit more involved in the political questions than Marx was. Marx was very interested in politics, but was more focused on the economic analysis, Engels more on the politics and the broader issues, or at least he wrote more about them. I think the important question for Marx, but even more for Engels, in the latter half of the 1800s, focused on the question of how to get beyond capitalism. Having exposed its contradictions, having exposed, as a critic should, the seamy side, the failed side, the dark side, the unjust side of capitalism, they convinced many others and themselves that you had to go beyond it. So the big question became how, how are we going to do that?

They made a decision that the key institution with which to accomplish a transition from capitalism to socialism/communism was the state. And it was the job of the workers to capture the state. Phrases like "the state is the executive committee of the ruling class" or "the state is what masterminds the society as a whole in the interests of the capitalists" mean that the great revolutionary strategy would be to mobilize workers to liberate the state from capitalist control. If the leadership that keeps the capitalist in control is replaced then society could be reorganized and redirected in an egalitarian and democratic manner. The mass of the people, the working class, could then make the transition from capitalism to socialism.

So the strategy became, "How do you capture the state?"

And the big debate among Marxists became, "Do you do that by violent revolutionary insurrection, or do you do it by slower, democratic, vote-getting, parliamentary activity?" Marxists disagreed on that and still do. From the end of Marx's writings in the 1880s right on to the present there are debates about which way to go by those who see the state as the focus of transitional strategies.

But one of the unfortunate and unforeseen consequences of this focus on the state, often attributed to Engels, is that you risk overvaluing the state, imagining that by capturing the state, you have made the key change, and that thereafter everything will more or less move to your socialist society. There I think you see one of the roots of the distortions and the failures afterwards. In the Soviet Union revolution of 1917 they did seize the state, Mao in China seized the state, Fidel in Cuba seized it state. And they discovered the morning after their revolutions that they still had huge tasks to accomplish. They also slowly discovered (consciously or, more often unconsciously) that if they did not make further, profound changes in their economic and political structures—including in the internal organization of producing units—then even with the power of the state, the post-revolutionary system they had established often could not survive.

To achieve socialism will require mutually reinforcing changes in many parts of society. It's not so important where you start. It's much more important that you understand the multidimensional, multilevel, multi-sector changes that are involved so that they all mutually reinforce one another in a new society rather than undoing one another and retreating back to capitalism.

I would argue that in the Soviet Union, for example, because they never changed the internal structure of the enterprise, workers were as alienated from their outputs in the Soviet Union as they had been in Russian private capitalism before. Soviet workers were as adversarially linked to the managers of their enterprises that were state officials as they had been before to the private officials. When the Soviet system experienced difficulties, as any system will, workers tended to blame the managers and the managers blamed the worker, thereby articulating the adversarial relation that had never been overcome inside Soviet enterprises. Eventually what the Soviet revolution did achieve was undone by the parts of society that the revolution could not change.

The same applies to Soviet households. In the early years of the revolution there were attempts to break from the old nuclear family and patriarchal household structure. And for ten years that was tried: communal kitchens, communal daycare, group living, all kinds of very interesting experiments in collective households. But when those experiments proved to be socially contentious and disruptive, Stalin shut them down at the end of the 1920s and reverted back to the classic Russian family and household structures. If you have your children growing up in a very unequal society, with the father very dominant, the mother very subordinate, it's going to be very hard to expect those people to be model citizens in a communist collective society. They have no experience of that at home, they have no implicit training for it. You would need to have a collective household to prepare people for a collective adulthood. That would have had to be discussed and debated and worked out in deliberate fashion—as it began to be in the early years. But that debate was shut down. And I would argue that the family, left in its old feudal, Russian patriarchal system, helped to undo the revolutionary changes of 1917.

When people who grew up in a very old family structure were introduced into a new enterprise, organization or society, sometimes they gave up their old ways and adopted the new one, but in many cases they broke and destroyed the new one because they were more comfortable in what was an old one. They gave to the factory manager the same respect they had been taught to have to father at home rather than seeing him as a fellow citizen. Very dangerous.

Capitalism understands that. It makes its schools teach the values that are useful to a capitalist system. Communist or socialist society would have to do the same in the schools and homes. Otherwise it's going to undo itself.

The Occupy movement was born on September 17, 2011. In 2012, as we go forward, how does Occupy expand?

I think the answer is to continue doing pretty much what it has been doing. The achievements of Occupy are absolutely stupendous, not only in American history but in any history. In its first few months Occupy has changed the political discourse in this country, pushed the right-wing Tea Party movement out of the headlines of this country (perhaps forever but certainly since September 2011), and made indignation with the injustices and corruption perpetrated by the 1 percent acceptable to articulate and express. That is unbelievable as a set of achievements. And to have done that in its first few months shows what has long been brewing just below the surface.

Occupy shows that across the country, in hundreds of cities, there are people who feel the same way are connecting and organizing. This does an inestimable job of teaching the American left, which is in fact large, that all of them who felt so alone in the 1970s, 1980s and 1990s aren't alone, that there are all kinds of people across the country able and willing to come out, participate, demonstrate, sleep overnight in a public park in a drafty tent, etc. It therefore gives strength, solidarity, unity, and a sense of community to working together to counter decades of economic injustice and the chronic recession of democracy.

The movement has also achieved a kind of psychological breakthrough of challenging power and the state and the corporate structures.

It's amazing. For fifty years in the U.S. we've had single-issue movements or ones drawn from sectors of the population who have spoken out against injustices experienced in their communities: African Americans, women, immigrants, people with sexual orientations different from the heterosexual norm, environmentalists, and others. Each of those movements sooner or later encountered the problem of capitalism and how it produced or sustained the problems they were seeking to overcome. However, with some exceptions, most hesitated to confront capitalism or make going beyond it a necessary part of their agendas for change. That seems too hard or too divisive to risk.

Occupy is a dramatic break from that. From the start, the movement has addressed the deplorable greed and injustice waged against the 99 percent by the capitalist system and the resulting displacement and suffering it has brought. Occupy represents the beginning of a historic shift in the United States. So my feeling is, "Wow, you are beginning to bring together very diverse interests into a real unity, you are beginning to give everyone on the left a sense of what is possible, you give everyone a sense on how powerful we can be, how much we can change, how daring we can be and still have all those social impacts. Wow!" As the movement transitions from tent encampments to organizing in new and creative ways, it moves its occupation deeper and deeper into national awareness through outreach, through direct democracy, through civil disobedience, through the creation of a movement-oriented media and an independent press.

But lastly, what I would stress most: the conditions that produced and drive the Occupy movement are not being offset, compensated or removed. The class war against the 99 percent continues. The political system, what some call the two-wings of one business party, will not create the opening in democracy necessary to turn things around. Plutocracy, rule of the rich, will spend lavishly to remain in control. Political dysfunction and economic dysfunction keep reinforcing one another. All of the corruption, corporate welfare and class war that drove the movement into being still exist.

Growing numbers no longer stand on the sidelines and listen to the cheerleaders praise the system as it attempts to take away jobs, homes and dignity. It's time to challenge the system and occupy the economy. Many Americans—with the Occupy movement as a dynamic example-in-progress—are ready to begin to move in genuinely new social directions.

Manifesto For Economic Democracy and Ecological Sanity

A new historical vista is opening before us in this time of change. Capitalism as a system has spawned deepening economic crisis alongside its bought-and-paid for political establishment. Neither serves the needs of our society. Whether it is secure, well-paid and meaningful jobs or a sustainable relationship with the natural environment that we depend on, our society is not delivering the results people need and deserve. We do not have the lives we want and our children's future is threatened because of social conditions that can and should be changed. One key cause for this intolerable state of affairs is the lack of genuine democracy in our economy as well as in our politics. One key solution is thus the institution of genuine economic democracy as the basis for a genuine political democracy as well. That means transforming the workplace in our society as we propose in what follows.

177

We are encouraged by The Occupy Wall Street (OWS) movement spreading across the United States and beyond. Not only does OWS express a widespread popular rejection of our system's social injustice and lack of democracy. OWS is also a movement for goals that include economic democracy. We welcome, support, and seek to build OWS as the urgently needed, broad movement to reorganize our society, to make our institutions accountable to the public will, and to establish both economic democracy and ecological sanity.

1) Capitalism and "delivering the goods"

Capitalism today abuses the people, environment, politics and culture in equal measures. It has fostered new extremes of wealth *and* poverty inside most countries, and such extremes always undermine or prevent democratic politics. Capitalist production for profit likewise endangers us by its global warming, widening pollution, and looming energy crisis. And now capitalism's recurrent instability (what others call the "business cycle") has plunged the world into the second massive global economic crisis in the last 75 years.

Yet both Republican and Democratic governments have failed to bring a recovery to the great mass of the American people. We continue to face high unemployment and home foreclosures alongside shrinking real wages, benefits and job security. Thus, increasing personal debt is required to secure basic needs. The government uses our taxes to bring recovery from the economic crisis to banks, stock markets, and major corporations. We have waited for bailouts of the corporate rich to trickle down to the rest of us; it never happened. To pay for their recovery we are told now to submit to cuts in public services, public employment, and even our Social Security and Medicare benefits. The budget deficits and national debts incurred to save capitalism from its own fundamental flaws are now used to justify shifting the cost of their recovery onto everyone else. We should not pay for capitalism's crisis and for the government's unjust and failed response to that crisis. It is time to take a different path, to make long-overdue economic, social and political changes.

We begin by drawing lessons from previous efforts to go beyond capitalism. Traditional socialism—as in the USSR—emphasized public instead of private ownership of means of production and government economic planning instead of markets. But that concentrated too much power in the government and thereby corrupted the socialist project. Yet the recent reversions back to capitalism neither overcame nor rectified the failures of Soviet-style socialism.

We have also learned from the last great capitalist crisis in the US during the1930s. Then an unprecedented upsurge of union organizing by the CIO and political mobilizations by Socialist and Communist parties won major reforms: establishing Social Security and unemployment insurance, creating and filling 11 million federal jobs. Very expensive reforms *in the middle of a depression* were paid for in part by heavily taxing corporations and the rich (who were also then heavily regulated). However, New Deal reforms were evaded, weakened or abolished in the decades after 1945. To increase their profits, major corporate shareholders and their boards of directors had every incentive to dismantle reforms. They used their profits to undo the New Deal. Reforms won will always remain insecure until workers who benefit from the reforms are in the position of receiving the profits of their enterprises and using them to extend, not undermine, those reforms.

The task facing us, therefore, goes well beyond choosing between private and public ownership and between markets and planning. Nor can we be content to re-enact reforms that capitalist enterprises can and will undermine. These are not our only alternatives. The strategy we propose is to establish a genuinely democratic basis—by means of reorganizing our productive enterprises—to support those reforms and that combination of property ownership and distribution of resources and products that best serve our social, cultural and ecological needs.

2) Economic Democracy at the Workplace and in Society

The change we propose—as a new and major addition to the agenda for social change—is to occur *inside production*: Inside the enterprises and other institutions (households, the state, schools, and so on) that produce and distribute the goods and services upon which society depends. Wherever production occurs, the workers must become collectively their own bosses, their own board of directors. Everyone's job description would change: in addition to your specific task, you would be required to participate fully in designing and running the enterprise. Decisions once made by private corporate boards of directors or state officials—what, how and where to produce and how to use the revenues received —would instead be made collectively and democratically by the workers themselves. Education would be redesigned to train all persons in the leadership and control functions now reserved for elites.

Such a reorganization of production would finally and genuinely subordinate the state to the people. The state's revenues (taxes, etc.) would depend on what the workers gave the state out of the revenues of the workers' enterprises. Instead of capitalists, a small minority, funding and thereby controlling the state, the majority—workers—would finally gain that crucial social position.

Of course, workplace democracy must intertwine with community democracy in the residential locations that are mutually interactive and interdependent with work locations. Economic and political democracy need and would reinforce one another. Self-directed workers and self-directed community residents must democratically share decision-making at both locations. Local, regional and national state institutions will henceforth incorporate shared democratic decision-making between workplace and residence based communities. Such institutions would draw upon the lessons of past capitalist and socialist experiences.

3) Benefits of Workplace Democracy

When workforce and residential communities decide together how the economy evolves, the results will differ sharply from the results of capitalism. Workplace democracy would not, for example, move production to other countries as capitalist corporations have done. Workers' self-directed enterprises would not pay a few top managers huge salaries and bonuses while most workers' paychecks and benefits stagnate. Worker-run enterprises sharing democratic decision-making with surrounding communities would not install toxic and dangerous technologies as capitalist enterprises often do to earn more profits. They would, however, be far more likely to provide daycare, elder care and other supportive services. For the first time in human history, societies could democratically rethink and re-organize the time they devote to work, play, relationships, and cultural activities. Instead of complaining that we lack time for the most meaningful parts of our lives, we could together decide to reduce labor time, to concentrate on the consumer goods we really need, and thereby to allow more time for the important relationships in our lives. We might thereby overcome the divisions and tensions (often defined in racial, gender, ethnic, religious, and other terms) that capitalism imposes on populations by splitting them into fully employed, partly employed, and contingent laborers, and those excluded from the labor market.

A new society can be built on the basis of democratically reorganizing our workplaces, where adults spend most of their lifetimes. Over recent centuries, the human community dispensed with kings, emperors and czars in favor of representative (and partly democratic) parliaments and congresses. The fears and warnings of disaster by those opposed to that social change were proved wrong by history. The change we advocate today takes democracy another necessary and logical step: into the workplace. Those who fear (and threaten) that it will not work will likewise be proven wrong.

4) An Immediate and Realistic Project

There are practical and popular steps we can take now toward realizing economic democracy. Against massive, wasteful and cruel unemployment and poverty, we propose a new kind of public works program. It would differ from the federal employment programs of the New Deal (when FDR hired millions of the unemployed) in two ways. First, it would focus on a "green" and support service agenda. By "green" we mean massively improving the sustainability of workplace and residential communities by, for example, building energy-saving mass transportation systems, restoring waterways, forests, etc., weatherizing residential and workplace structures and establishing systematic anti-pollution programs. By "support service" we mean new programs of children's day-care and elder-care to help all families coping with the conditions of work and demographics in the US today.

However, the new kind of pubic works program we propose would differ even more dramatically from all past public works projects. Instead of paying a weekly dole to the unemployed, our public works program would emphasize *providing the unemployed with the funds to begin and build their own cooperative, self-directed democratic enterprises.*

The gains from this project are many. The ecological benefits alone would make this the most massive environmental program in US history. Economic benefits would be huge as millions of citizens restore self-esteem damaged by unemployment and earn incomes enabling them to keep their homes and, by their purchases, provide jobs to others. Public employment at decent pay for all would go a long way toward lessening the gender, racial, and other job discriminations now dividing our people.

A special benefit would be a new freedom of choice for Americans. As a people, we could see, examine and evaluate the benefits of working inside enterprises where every worker is both employee and employer, where decisions are debated and decided democratically. For the first time in US history, we will begin to enjoy this freedom of choice: working in a top-down, hierarchically organized capitalist corporation or working in a cooperative, democratic workplace. The future of our society will then depend on how Americans make that choice, and that is how the future of a democratic society should be determined.

5) The Rich Roots Sustaining this Project

Americans have been interested in and built various kinds of cooperative enterprises—more or less *non-capitalist* enterprises—throughout our history. The idea of building a "cooperative commonwealth" has repeatedly attracted many. Today, an estimated 13.7 million Americans work in 11,400 *Employee Stock Ownership Plan companies* (ESOPs), in which employees own part or all of those companies. So-called "not-for-profit" enterprises abound across the US in many different fields. Some alternative, *non-capitalist* enterprises are inspired by the example of *Mondragon*, a federation of over 250 democratically-run worker cooperatives employing 100,000 based in Spain's Basque region. Since their wages are determined by the worker-owners themselves, the ratio between the wages of those with mostly executive functions and others average 5:1 as compared to the 475:1 in contemporary capitalist multinational corporations.

The US cooperative movement stretches today from the *Arizmendi Association* (San Francisco Bay) to the *Vida Verde Cleaning Cooperative* (Massachusetts) to *Black Star Collective Pub and Brewery* (Austin, Texas), to name just a few. The largest conglomerate of worker owned co-operatives in the U.S. is the "Evergreen Cooperative Model" (or "Cleveland Model"), consisting, e.g. of the *Evergreen Cooperative Laundry* (ECL), the *Ohio Cooperative Solar* (OCS) and the *Green City Growers*. These cooperatives share a) common ownership and democracy at the workplace; b) ecological commitments to produce sustainable goods and services and create "green jobs", and c) new kinds of communal economic planning, mediated by "anchor institutions" (e.g. universities, non-profit hospitals), community foundations, development funds, state-owned banks or employee ownership banks etc. Such cooperatives are generating new concepts and kinds of economic development.

These examples' varying kinds and degrees of democracy in the workplace all attest to an immense social basis of interest in and commitment to non-capitalist forms of work. Contrary to much popular mythology, there is a solid popular base for a movement to expand and diversify the options for organizing production. Workplace democracy responds to deep needs and desires.

About the Authors

David Barsamian, one of America's most tireless and wide-ranging journalists, has altered the independent media landscape his weekly syndicated program Alternative Radio—begun in 1986. He is author of many books with Noam Chomsky, Howard Zinn, Tariq Ali, Edward Said, Eqbal Ahmad, and Arundhati Roy. His articles and interviews appear in the *Progessive*, *Z*, *The Sun*, and other magazines and journals. His web page is www.alternativeradio.org

Richard D. Wolff is Professor of Economics Emeritus, University of Massachusetts, Amherst. He is currently a Visiting Professor in the Graduate Program in International Affairs of the New School University in New York. Wolff has also taught economics at Yale University, City University of New York, University of Paris I (Sorbonne) and The Brecht Forum in New York City. Wolff is author of *Capitalism Hits the Fan: The Global Economic Meltdown and What to Do About It*. Wolff hosts the weekly hour-long radio program *Economic Update* on WBAI, 99.5 FM, New York City. He writes regularly for the *Guardian*, Truthout.org and the MRZine. His website is rdwolff.com.

RECENT AND FORTHCOMING TITLES IN THE OPEN MEDIA SERIES

Making the Future: Occupations, Interventions, Empire and Resistance
by Noam Chomsky

The Historic Unfulfilled Promise
by Howard Zinn

The Meaning of Freedom
by Angela Y. Davis

National Insecurity
The Cost of American Militarism
By Melvin A. Goodman

Targeting Iran
Interviews with David Barsamian

To Die in Mexico:
Dispatches from Inside the Drug War
by John Gibler

Dying To Live: A Story of U.S. Immigration in an Age of Global Apartheid
by Joseph Nevins, photography by Mizue Aizeki

Open Media is a movement-oriented publishing project committed to the vision of "one world in which many worlds fit"—a world with social justice, democracy, and human rights for all people. Founded in 1991 by Greg Ruggiero, Open Media has a history of producing critically acclaimed and best-selling titles that address the most urgent political and social issues of our time.

City Lights Open Media Series
www.citylights.com/collections/openmedia/